# MAKING MONEY

## IS NOT ILLEGAL IMMORAL OR FATTENING

ART FREEDMAN
&
BRUCE SANDERS

# DEDICATIONS

A good part of my life as this book is being written is to get on an airplane nearly every week and fly somewhere in the world. I'm in front of retailers most every week with one very specific purpose in mind. I want to do every thing I can to help small business retailers succeed in what has become a very challenging proposition. I want my grandchildren to have the opportunity to own and operate a small business if this is their choice. What I work hard to do is reenergize, educate, and inspire retailers to go beyond where they ever thought possible in their businesses. I call this retailer-to-retailer education. I'm very proud to have this opportunity, and I do not treat this responsibility lightly.

As you can imagine, I'm away from home more than I am there. This can be very tough at times. This book allows me the opportunity to help others make more money in their businesses and also to thank those who have made this all possible.

- My wife of 39 years, Geni, for her patience, love, understanding, support, and accepting the responsibility to run our business.
- Our children, Eric and Shere, Jill and Dan for their involvement and dedication to the business and support of their mom. And for six incredible grandkids (soon to be seven).
- Homer Nelson. We used to ride bikes five to six times a week. Now we are down to five or six times a year. Sorry, buddy. "The toughest part of any challenge is just pushing the GO button."

- Ray Griffith for his belief that I had the knowledge, desire, and ability to educate others. And for allowing me to do so.
- Bruce Sanders. My business partner and brother-in-law. Believe me, without Bruce, this book would never have happened.

Art Freedman
Retail In Motion, LLC
art@retailinmotion.us
April 2009

Reading this book will give you a sense of Art's devotion to building the success of small to midsize retail businesses. But unless you've actually been around Art for a while, this book can give you only a taste of his spirited optimism towards retailing and towards life in general. As Art will tell you himself, though, his optimism is more a matter of "You can do it" than "Just relax, since everything will work out." It's optimism conditioned on hard work and with little patience for complaining.

That came through clearly a few New Year's eves ago when a prolonged rainstorm caused the creek across from my home to overflow its banks. The flooding destroyed decades worth of photo albums stored in our garage and sentenced our family cars to the junkyard. When Irene—who is my wife, Art's sister, and a world-contender optimist herself—told Art about what had happened, Art shot back with, "Have any crocodiles gotten into the house yet?" and then improvised around that theme for a minute or two to cover the topics of rats, freshwater stingrays, and poisonous snakes.

Nope, Art, we didn't have any of those, and nobody was injured. Irene and I stopped complaining and got back to shoveling California adobe mud.

Now add to the hard-nosed optimism a generous dose of generosity. Art is firmly convinced that the riches he has worked diligently to earn in his life are best enjoyed by sharing them with family, friends, and fellow retailers.

Art showed that generosity in allowing me the opportunity to work with his words and stories as he and I collaborated in producing this book.

Retailer optimism. Retailer generosity. Retailer success. Those are perfectly exemplified by Art Freedman, and it is to those three I dedicate my contributions to this book. And, oh yes, to Irene, who first introduced me to her kid brother and for years has encouraged my search as a psychologist for the truths of why people buy.

Bruce Sanders, Ph.D., SPHR
Retail In Motion, LLC
bruce@retailinmotion.us
April 2009

# FOREWORD

Art Freedman speaks retailer-to-retailer. He's run his own stores, and earlier in his career, he worked in retail stores owned by others, so he has the hands-on experience. He's come from the trenches. That is what makes Art's words of advice so valuable and so credible. He knows what works very well and what doesn't work so well. This is not somebody expounding theory. Art has put it all to the test.

All of this is why when Art talks, retailers love to listen. Art also is highly engaging. What accompanies his excellent advice is a way of sharing it that gets retailers involved and keeps them involved. I consult with retailers from around the world in many different sorts of countries and cultures. I find that there are far more similarities than differences in retailing, whether you are in Australia, South Africa, Saudi Arabia, Indonesia, or the U.S. One sign of that is how Art engages the interest of retailers from every one of those countries and many more.

I think I know how you work, retailer, so I'd be surprised if you take the time to sit down somewhere and read this book cover to cover. Still, if you open this book to any page and start reading, I think you'll keep reading because of Art's engaging style and the way his collaborator, Bruce Sanders, edited and enriched Art's words. When you put down the book, it will be only because you are so excited to take Art's ideas into action in order to improve your profitability and remember the joy there is in successful retailing.

Art says to take a few ideas and start with them. He says that if you are feeling a bit overwhelmed by his talk of item segmentation, item price thresholds, and item velocity, then you can begin with his specific instructions for price rounding. I can tell you from personal experience that his philosophy and presentation on rounding are right on target. Those retailers I know who have implemented Art's rounding tactics have seen immediate bottom-line improvements.

Art also talks about the value in retaining customers and says that retailers who increase their prices must earn that right by delivering what Art and Bruce call Boomerang Customer Service, where the customers come back soon and often. This whole idea of the importance of retaining customers isn't attended to often enough. Some of my consultation with retailers amounts to bringing them from practices found in third-world countries to retailing practices of the 21st Century. A part of that is giving real meaning to engaging the customer. I've told you about how skilled Art is in engaging retailers, and I think there is something to be learned from this about the importance of retailers engaging their customers.

Whenever retailers have their psyches stuck in practices from the past, a big danger is that they don't appreciate the value of a customer. I think about how I've seen that affect returns and exchanges. A customer will come into the store with an item to return, and the salesperson will treat the customer with suspicion rather than servicing the customer. "Why are you returning this? What's wrong with it? The product wasn't like this when you left the store with it."

If there is one idea I might add to the richness of "golden nuggets" Art serves up, it is my recommendation that you have a return and exchange policy in your store which is as clearly stated as it can be. Include in this policy, "We guarantee your satisfaction" and "Your receipt gives you the right to return whatever you buy here." Then, as Art would say, SHOUT IT OUT. Post the policy and make sure every staff member is familiar with it and follows the policy.

Don't think I'm saying to be soft in your business dealings. I like the writings of Jack Welch, former Chairman and CEO of General Electric, because of his practical, no-nonsense approach to business. He shows us how sticking to the fundamentals is important. He reminds us that one of the top fundamentals is the people. Art Freedman says, "The older I get, the less I need to know and the more I need to know who does know." Jack Welch wrote, "My main job was developing talent. I was a gardener providing water and other nourishment to our top 750 people." Then Mr. Welch added, "Of course, I had to pull out some weeds, too."

Have the right people in place and see that those people have the right resources to do their jobs. In his best-selling book, *Good to Great*, organizational researcher Jim Collins wrote about "getting the right people on the bus." In retailing, we must have the right people and manage to their strengths. This means having enough people. Retailers always want to keep down headcounts because staffing is such a large part of expenses. But you cannot shrink yourself to greatness. In tough times, you might need to take a couple of steps backwards, but be sure that over time you always keep still moving forward.

*Making Money Is Not Illegal Immoral, or Fattening*, the book you are now holding in your hands, retailer, is in the class with Jack Welch's and Jim Collins' books. You'll be given practical, specific, no-nonsense tactics. If you sneak a look at the very end of this book, you will see that Art and Bruce send you off with, "Go out there and make more money." So please allow me to send you on by saying, "Go to it now and start reading about how to make more money."

Murray Armstrong
President
Ace Hardware International
April 2009

# CHAPTER 1:
# MAKING MONEY IS NOT ILLEGAL, IMMORAL, OR FATTENING

*A thing is worth whatever the buyer will pay for it.*
Publilius Syrus
(1st Century B.C.)

Thank you for opening this book to read it, and I really mean that. I'm sensitive to your time. I'm a retailer just like you. My family owns and operates American River Ace Hardware in Folsom, California. I know that retailers are time-starved. We never really complete everything we start on. We always have to-do lists, and they just go from one day to another. So I know clearly that as a result of you taking the time to read this book, there are things in your store that won't get done as soon, and you're going to have to play catch-up each time you get back to the business.

It is very important to me that as you read this book, you can pull out tactics that you'll be able to put into action immediately to make more money. I call those tactics "golden nuggets." So read a chapter or two at a time, pull out a golden nugget or two, think about the nuggets, and then put the nuggets into action.

I think I've done every single job that anybody has in a retail store. I started out in retail like a lot of retailers have, on the floor, sweeping and cleaning and all that, and I worked my way up. I ran departments, I ran stores, I ran groups of stores, I ran half the whole state of California for a large home center chain. I got involved in marketing, in display, in sourcing or ranging products, in leading people, the same things that many of you do. Then in 1988, I decided the corporate world was no longer for me. The corporate world was not something I wanted to do any longer. That's when my family and I started our own business, an Ace Hardware store. (Ace Hardware Corporation is a co-op. Each Ace Hardware store is independently owned and operated.)

In the Sacramento, California market, where my family's store is located, we compete with Home Depot and Lowe's. They are very strong retailers. We've had to compete against Home Depot significantly in the Sacramento market since the 1990's, so I've been competing against Home Depot for a long part of my life, and, frankly, we've competed against them very successfully. As for Lowe's, they are an extremely strong competitor, real tough, like an upgraded Home Depot store, more customer-friendly, more women-friendly, mellower colors.

One of the founders of Home Depot is Bernie Marcus. Bernie Marcus came to an Ace Hardware convention some years back and that day stood up in front of maybe 3,000 to 4,000 people in a room. Bernie Marcus said to all of the Ace Hardware store retailers, "There will always be room in the market for the Big Boxes and room for a convenient hardware store."

We all cheered loudly, "Yeah!" But Bernie Marcus is a very, very smart man, and he chose his words on that day very, very well. He said, "a convenient hardware store." Just one convenient hardware store in each market. Bernie Marcus did not say, "a bunch of convenient hardware stores." And that is exactly what is turning out to be true. The cream has risen to the top. The great retailers just flat figure it out. The great retailers can compete against a Home Depot, a Lowe's, a Bunning's or anybody else you put in their marketplace. It doesn't matter. They're *great* at what they do because *good* is no longer enough in many markets.

Over the years, nearly every successful, regional hardware, home center, and lumber yard chain that operated on the West Coast has been in Sacramento. It's been one of the largest growth areas of California for as long as I can remember.

We've had companies like Handyman Home Centers, where I worked for 13 years. We had a company called Payless Cashways. They operated multiple stores and were a huge retailer in the 60's, 70's, 80's. They are gone. We've had Pay'N'Pack. We had Ace Plumbing and Electrical, which had no relation to Ace Hardware. We had a lot of True Value stores. We had a lot of independent hardware stores.

Now if you fast-forward to today, what you have in the Sacramento market and most of the surrounding area is a large contingent of Home Depots and Lowe's stores, and you have a fairly large contingent of Ace Hardware stores, a few Orchard Supply stores, and that's pretty much it. Everybody else is gone. Most of the regional and national players that were in Sacramento are gone.

They didn't go away because they were making too much money, I promise you that. They lost a *lot* of money, they were no longer important to the consumer, and they disappeared. We used to have a company called Newbert's. They were a huge independent in Sacramento. Anybody who lived in the Sacramento region knew about Newbert's. They're gone. We had a company called Brown's Hardware. If you couldn't find it anywhere else, you went down to Brown's Hardware, and that's who had it. There was a guy sitting at the front counter who could find anything you wanted in the store. And you know what? They're gone. They're all gone.

What we've got left in Sacramento and our surrounding area is a strong group of Ace Hardware stores. There are actually 58 of us, and we work very, very closely together in the Northern California, Nevada, and Idaho markets. I'll tell you what brought us together, and I'll tell you when it brought us together. In the 1990's, Home Depot was hammering away at us. They were absolutely killing us, and what brings independent hardware dealers together? Fear. We were scared to death of what was going on. The independents were disappearing, the True Values were disappearing, we had some of our own stores disappearing, and we didn't know what was going to happen.

So we came together. It was a Friday afternoon. There were eleven of us in that room. We sat around the table, and by the way, most of those eleven people who sat together at that table are still very close, very good friends, even these many years later. We sat together and looked at each other and said, "What are we going to do?" Then we started marketing together, we started doing all of our advertising together, we started trading information together, and it really was clearly us against them. This is the day we went from being competitors to being partners.

We've done better than many others. Ace Hardware Corporation is an 85-year-old company that's been very good at wholesale and good at helping their retailers at retail, but Ace retailers have been falling off the earth every single day. Ace Hardware Corporation's volume increased, but the store count was dropping. The stores that were going out of business were being replaced by better and stronger Ace retailers.

Our coming together in the Sacramento area worked tremendously for us, and maybe it could work tremendously for you. But one thing I'd never tell you is that what I do in my business or what somebody else does in their business is *always* the very best way for *you* to do business. I'm not stupid enough to think that. All I'm going to do is give you ideas, golden nuggets, that you can use in your store and execute and make more money in your business. That's the whole purpose for you reading this book, and I'll tell you this: If you don't do anything as a result of reading this book, we have effectively wasted your time, and I would not, in a million years, ask a retailer to waste their time. I know it is too valuable.

I've lots of ideas to share, and I realize this can be overwhelming. Some of you will say this is so much stuff. So I want to set your mind at ease a little bit. I want you to know how I look at something like this. I look at this as an opportunity to get a few nuggets for your business. Not a thousand nuggets, not a hundred. I'd like you to take maybe three things away to start. I'm only asking you to come away with three tactics, three things you're going to do when you get back to overseeing your business.

Something else I want you to know about my approach: I'm not into creating warm and fuzzies. Don't expect me to tell you that retailing is wonderful, don't ever worry about anything, you'll be fine. You most definitely will *not* hear that from me because anybody that I go and listen to that tells me everything is fine and everything is rosy, I stop listening to them as soon as they say that because that's different from the world I know is out there, the world I know about. I do not talk to make retailers feel good. I talk to get retailers to make changes so they can make more money. This is what I have always referred to as "teaching and preaching."

Still, when you read what I'm telling you here, you might think at first that I'm a complete idiot. Hey, I have no problem with you considering me to be a complete idiot for now and then calling me a complete idiot next time we meet. I'm not offended. But what I'm going to ask you to do is to suspend judgment until you *think about* and then maybe *try out* the nuggets. Would you just think about it before you say it's a stupid idea? Think about how it is relevant to your business or not relevant to your business. Talk to some of the people who are in your store. Then make an informed decision about which ones to do. Then *do them*.

When you're done reading this book, how will you decide if it's been time well spent? Number one, decide if you know more than you did before. Number two, are you doing things differently? Maybe not a whole bunch of things to start, but at least a few things. Will you do hundreds of things differently? No, you're not. I would never expect you to. I can't. I read an entire book, and I get one, two, three nuggets.

That's why so few retailers read books on how to improve their businesses. It's because they don't see value in the entire book. Value in the entire book? I read an entire book, and all I want is one good idea because that's all I can deal with. Otherwise, I'm going to forget the rest of the stuff. So please do just a few things differently. Do them well, and that will make the time you've spent reading this book worthwhile.

But the real test is this: When you take action, at the end of the day, do you make more money? If Bruce Sanders, my business partner in Retail In Motion, LLC (www.retailinmotion.us) and my collaborator in this book, and I can't make you more money, we've wasted your time. Do you want to make more money this year than you made last year? I don't think you're going to say, "No, I made so much money last year that I don't want to make any more money this year because I have to pay more fees to the bank when I deposit more money."

So please do us a favor by repeating this after me: "Making money is not illegal, it's not immoral, it's not fattening. It's okay to make money. And you know what? It's okay to make a lot of money. There is nothing wrong with it."

Doesn't it feel really good to say that?

There are retailers who think they're ripping off the customers if they're making money. There are people who are afraid of making money. Home Depot is not afraid of making money. Lowe's is not afraid of making money. I'm certainly not afraid of making money. Some people have just got to be going, "Oh, okay, I thought if I had enough money in the bank to cover the bills coming in, we were okay." If you told me that was your attitude, I would look at you straight up and here is what I'd say to you, "You are going out of business at least a little bit every day. You just don't know it. It will catch up to you eventually in a competitive market."

I would sit there for hours to talk to you about the importance of operating your business as if a Big Box were going to open next door to you tomorrow. Don't wait for a Big Box to come in next to you. A whole lot of retailers are out of business today because they took the, "We'll just wait and see what happens" kind of attitude. I need to make you some more money NOW.

No warm and fuzzies. Bruce and I have one clear objective for this book: To improve your profitability as a retailer. Making money and turning that money into profitability is not illegal. It is not immoral. It is not fattening. It's okay to make money. It's okay to make *lots* of money. My job is to make you more money, and I love my job.

# GOLDEN NUGGETS FOR NOW

- Each day, remind yourself that making money is not illegal, it's not immoral, it's not fattening. It's okay to make money. And you know what? It's okay to make a lot of money.
- Operate your business as if a Big Box were going to open next door to you tomorrow.
- Decide if you are a great retailer, who creates thousands of opportunities to succeed, or a weak retailer, who blames someone else for any failures.

# CHAPTER 2:
# YOU ARE IN BUSINESS
# TO MAKE MONEY

*The actual price at which any commodity is commonly
sold is called its market price. It may either be above, or
below, or exactly the same with its natural price.*
Adam Smith (1776)

Why are you in business? There is only one good answer
to that question: To make money.

Sometimes when I ask retailers that question, I get,
"We're in business to support the community." But for how
long can you support the community if you are not making
any money? Some people say, "We are in business to support our employees and their families." I say, "Well, that's a
wonderful thing. But for how long can you support them if
you're not turning a profit?" How many families did Handyman Home Center support? They had about 300 stores.
They're all gone. The home center hardware and lumber-
yard, retailer of the year in 1984 in the United States was a
company called Heckinger's. If you read anything about
Heckinger's in 1985, you'd think they walked on water.
They're gone. How many families do they support now?
None.

Do you know why they're not here any more? They lost
one heck of a lot of money, and they went out of business.
There is only one reason why you are in business, and that is

to make money. This model is working in the United States, and it's working very well: Make money in your business, and take a portion of that, maybe two-thirds of the profits, to reinvest in your store. The first third goes to the store owner for what they risk on that business, and I don't take that lightly. I've got personal guarantees out there just like a lot of you do. Everything I own is at stake when I sign a personal guarantee. I don't take it lightly, and I wouldn't want other retailers to take it lightly either.

So you reinvest two-thirds back into the business, and you make more money, and you reinvest two-thirds of that back into the business, you make more money, and so on. That model is working. But one problem is that Home Depot and Lowes have successfully over the last few years put 7% to 10% to the bottom line before taxes. You could do the math. If you did $50 to $90 billion and you put this much to the bottom line, you're making a lot of money. A typical hardware store puts about 3% to the bottom line, yes, only 3%, and part of that is a rebate they aren't ever going to see until they sell the business. How do you compete when you're making no more than one-third as much as your competition? But more important than that is how are you going to compete if they're reinvesting in their business and you're not? Well, the answer to that is really simple. You can't. Over time, they will rip you apart, and they'll do it just a little bit every single day.

There are four areas of your life where every single day, you either get just a little bit better or a little bit worse. Nobody stays the same. The first area is your health. Every single day, you either get less healthy or more healthy. The second is your personal development. Every single day, you forget things. Every day. Proven fact. So the only question is do you learn new things every day or when you go to bed at night, are you dumber than when you woke up in the morning? That's the way it is. We have to take it upon ourselves. At your level, you are responsible for your learning. You don't have anyone else to blame if you don't learn something. People who work for you in the stores, you need to help them out a little bit, but at this level, it's all on your back. But wait a second here. You're reading this book. So you are attending to your personal development.

The third area in which you either get better or get worse each day is your family life. It is the relationships with those closest to you and also includes your family finances. They either become stronger or weaker every single day. It's just a little bit, but over time, it's a lot.

The fourth area is the world you and I live in—the business world. Your business either gets a little bit better or a little bit worse every day. Your business won't be the same today as it was yesterday. The way that Home Depot got to where they are is that every single time they opened up a new store, they got a little bit better and a little bit better and a little bit better. Every single time they put an ad out on the street, they learned from their mistakes, tweaked it, and made it a little bit better. Every single part of their business, they looked to get just a little bit better over time. Home Depot, Lowe's, Wal-Mart. These people understand how to make money.

Now imagine that the next time you start to walk into your store, I walk up behind you, put my hand on your shoulder, and ask you, "What are you going to do to make a difference in here today?"

I expect an answer. Remember, no warm and fuzzies. I don't want you looking back at me like Bambi caught in the headlights. I'll be mighty disappointed if you say, "I'm not sure" or "Gee, I never thought about it." I want to know exactly what you are going to do. If I stopped my store manager right there at the opening in the morning, and I put my hand on his shoulder and said, "What are we going to do in here today to make a difference?," my store manager had better have a whole list of things, and it better not be, "Let me go inside and check my notes from yesterday." What are we going to do to be better *today*, and let's know it *before* we walk into the store, because once we walk in, we've got all kinds of distractions to handle.

That's the start of the day. How about at the end of your day? When you go to bed tonight, you know your head's going to hit the pillow and some of you are going to do what I probably do and you kind of think about what you did during the day. So when that happens to you tonight, think about this: What did you do to make a difference in your world?

I'm not talking about grand strategies. I'm talking about specific nuggets. Here's an example: About 80% of all batteries are sold on impulse. Now what does that mean to you? Well, I was in a store, and they didn't have any batteries up by the check stands. They're getting only 20% of the total battery sales that they could be getting. So that's a nugget. You just grab hold of it and decide what you want to do with it.

Here's another one: When you get back to your store, stand in front, right where your doors are, and walk into your store fifteen feet. Then turn around and look behind you. What you are looking at right there is what many customers don't even see. They don't acclimate until they get inside of your store for about fifteen feet. If you can, and I know it may not be realistic in some stores, if you have a product that's displayed in those first fifteen feet, duplicate it where its proper location is in the store.

One key is knowing the nuggets, but the real key is implementing them. When retailers are doing well financially, it's hard to get them to change how they do things. There are successful retailers I've worked with, where I'll show them how to pick up $40,000 or $50,000 or even $100,000, but they won't do it. The reason they won't do it is they've already got a lot of money, and getting more money doesn't mean that much to them. They're missing the opportunities.

Even if you're hurting financially, you might not be hurting enough to put in the energy necessary to make more money. The money alone is not a good motivator. I'll bet that you're not wondering whether you'll get a meal tonight. I'll bet you have clothes in your closet, some kind of transportation, and a roof over your head. But if you don't open up your mind to making more money, you're missing the opportunities. Money is only paper without a plan what to do with it.

With some retailers, every time I suggest a nugget, they think about the exceptions, where it might not work. I know that there are exceptions to almost everything. But if you deal just with exceptions in your world, you won't do anything. You won't be able to move ahead quickly enough for retailing success. I like to take action which is based on what is true most of the time, not on exceptions. And I will not wait until I have every piece of information possible to make a decision. When I have about 70%, I'm moving.

When we have an exception and we're pulled off track, and then we get another exception and we're pulled off in another direction, let's quickly handle the exceptions and get back on track. If I really wanted to get your feathers up, get you so you'd start disagreeing with me, I'd say my opinion is with anything that comes back for a refund in the store, give the refund, take care of the customer. Now you go, "Two years ago, I had somebody steal a drill. You mean I'm going to take care of that guy?" Then I ask, "How many refunds do you do in your store?" "Well, we do a whole bunch." So isn't what happened with the drill an exception? Just deal with it and move on. Don't let that be the only thing you remember about refunds, please. Do not ever let one customer impact the way you think about all customers.

I was working with a retailer who told me, "I agree with everything you said except this one thing about taking care of customers on refunds." And I said, "Rob, how much volume do you do?" Well, Rob does a good job. He's a great retailer. A multimillion dollar business. I said, "Rob, what percentage of those sales are a problem where you say maybe somebody took advantage of you a little bit?" He replied, "I don't know, about $30,000 a year." I said "That's about two-tenths of one percent of your business. Let's walk through your store and find some areas where you can pick up 2 to 3 to 4 margin points in your business, and then let's forget about the bad refunds. Let's not dwell on it. Let's dwell on the things where we can really make an impact in your business."

## GOLDEN NUGGETS FOR NOW

- Each day, remind yourself why you are in business: To make money.
- As you make money in your business, take about two-thirds of the profits to reinvest in your store.
- At the start of each day and again at the end of each day, take stock of how you are getting better (or worse?).
- Stock batteries by your check stands.
- Walk into your store from the front and continue about fifteen feet. Then turn around and look behind you. If you have a product that's displayed in those first fifteen feet, duplicate it where its proper location is in the store.
- Remind yourself that money is only paper without a plan what to do with it.
- When you have about 70% of the information you need in order to make a decision, then start moving on the decision.
- Do not ever let one customer impact the way you think about all customers.

# CHAPTER 3:
# KEEP THE RIGHT ATTITUDE

*What we obtain too cheaply we esteem too lightly; it is dearness only which gives everything its value.*
Thomas Paine (1786)

Why do you need to be more profitable? First of all, you can't compete in a competitive market if you're not profitable. You must have inventory to support customer demand. You must grow your business, and I understand growing your business is not necessarily opening up more stores. It also can mean growing with your people, growing with your categories. It is making your business a little bit better every day.

You need a succession plan, and that's much easier when you are profitable. What happens when you have no succession plan, and the owner/operator passes away? Profitability increases the market value of your business. Profitability helps you get high-quality staff. And my favorite: The more money you make, the more time you have for your family and yourself.

I was working with a retailer in California, a $6 or $7 million retailer. Well, I do the math. An average hardware store owner should take home in salary about 5% of their top line sales. If they have multiple stores, that changes, and that doesn't include bottom-line profit. So you tell me a retailer is doing $7 million, and I can probably live on $350,000 for a couple of years before I have to build that business up.

I asked the retailer, "What are you going to do with your business?" What I meant was, what would happen at the point where the owner retired. He replied, "I don't know."

That's a fairly common answer when I ask that question. I said, "Do you have any kids?" He said, "Yes, I have two kids, a daughter who is an EMT and a son who's an engineer." "Why aren't they interested in the business?" "Well, they watched their mom and me work in the business six to seven days a week year after year, and we never really had a whole lot of money, and we missed a lot of soccer games and meetings, and they just didn't want the same life."

That makes sense. I wouldn't want it either. But it's a problem. When kids coming up through the business don't see the parents' business allowing them to do what they like to do and have enough time for the family, they don't want any part of it.

So you want profitability for family reasons, succession planning, and more. From another side of this, you want to avoid poor cash flow. Retailing is a cash flow business. I don't care what the profit and loss statements say, and believe me, I read lots of them. What I want to know is whether there is money in the bank or if there is not money in the bank, why not. If there is money in the bank, why is it there? I want to know where the money is going in a business.

What do retailers tend to do when a bill comes in for a dollar and there isn't a dollar in the bank? In many cases, the retailer takes money that should have been used to replenish inventory and pays expenses with it. Next in line is likely to be cutting payroll, and then slashing away at training and advertising. The four things that we absolutely need to do to compete when we have cash flow problems, we don't do. Just what we must have in challenging economic circumstances, we cut.

Most retailers that I work with don't know that they're using money that should go to inventory to pay expenses because they just don't understand the mathematics of margin and expenses. But if you don't have it, you can't sell it. You must be in stock. That's a top priority. I would argue all

day long there's very little in the business that's more important than staying in stock once the store is up and running
out of the ground. Very close behind that, and this is where
I would get you to start to think, is the interaction between
your customers and your employees. I mean right there
where they interact, where they're talking on the floor. So
how much of your time do you spend every day coaching
the people who work for you in your store to do a better job
taking care of the customers?

Is your answer, "Well, I trained each of them when I
hired them"? If you said that to me, I'd fall down on the
floor laughing. How in the world can you train an hourly
employee once and think they are going to go out on the
floor and do it right all the time? It isn't going to happen.
So I want to convince you to spend enough time out on
the floor coaching the people who work for you to do a
better job dealing with the customers. That will be part of
your competitive advantage. With Home Depot, customer
service is an extremely low priority, somewhere below keeping the store manager's shoes shined. The spin that Home
Depot puts on it is, "We spend millions of dollars on training."
Well, if your turnover of employees was as high as it is at
Home Depot, you'd spend a great deal of money on training, too. They have a difficult time keeping their employees in the stores. At Lowe's, it's better, but they don't have
enough employees or spend enough money on payroll to
be able to service customers well.

What do I base that on? A while back, I joined a small
team of Ace Hardware people to visit and review Ace
Hardware, Home Depot, Lowe's, and Menard's stores all
over America. Menard's stores are mostly in the Midwest
states. Instead of 100,000 square foot stores, like a typical
Home Depot or Lowe's, Menard's newer stores are 250,000
square feet. They have an unbelievable range of product.
Menard's is the toughest retailer out there in competitive
retail pricing.

Our team did a lot of research. We were trying to figure
out why it was that we had some Ace Hardware stores in

very competitive markets that were failing, yet others were doing very well. Based on that research, we identified four top threads that made the difference between failure and success.

If you give me a competitive market where the Big Boxes are close to the Ace retailer, and we visited many of those, I'll tell you a few things about the retailer who not only survives, but thrives. I don't even need to go see the store. First, the owner/operator is investing money in his business. I'm sure of that because in a competitive market, if you don't reinvest in your business, the Big Box gets a little bit better every day, you get a little bit worse, and, over time, that gap really widens.

## Top Four Threads of Success

1. Money because you must reinvest in your business

2. Inventory because our customers expect us to be in stock

3. Leadership because you direct the success of your business

4. Attitude because your business is all about you

Second, the retailer who does well against the Big Boxes understands the importance of a replenishment system. They understand the customer is looking for inventory, so the store has inventory. The third crucial difference between those who do well and those who don't is the winners have outstanding leadership in the business. When I predict the impact of a Big Box coming into the market, I will tweak the numbers, our sales numbers, by about 15% up or down based on the leader of the business.

I used to think that the best retailers owned stores. How far from the truth that is! The best retailers, unfortunately, don't run stores, they don't own stores. Instead, they work for other companies, and they're making lots of money, tremendous amounts of money. Often, the ones who own the stores are there because they inherited them. They are there because their mom or dad started the business. Could be they got there because they really liked plumbing or they really liked electrical and they wanted to get in there and sell. Maybe they ended up there because they were not able to work for anybody else, they rebelled against following instructions from job supervisors outside family employment. I have a nickname for a family member who is employed only because they are family. I call them COO's, not for Chief Operating Officer, but for Child of Owner. I recall asking one COO what was the advantage of working in the family business. His answer? "Job security." Business owners who come into our industry because of their experience in construction or maybe because they were a plumbing contractor do not usually do well at making money. They may have good product knowledge, but little to no sense of how to make money.

Now however you got where you are, as the owner/operator of a small to midsize business, chances are you haven't received all the training you could use in empowering employees, cultivating trust, building teamwork, using strategy, practicing resourcefulness, and projecting a professional attitude. All of that goes into retailer leadership.

One owner/operator I know has two adult children in his retail business, but those two kids are going to grow up knowing only what he knows because he does not let those kids get training outside the environment of the family store. That makes it much tougher for their store to realize the tremendous profit-making benefits of great retailer leadership.

## Six Components of Retailer Leadership

1. Empowering employees
2. Cultivating trust
3. Building teamwork
4. Using strategy
5. Practicing resourcefulness
6. Projecting a professional attitude

Number four on the "Top Four Threads of Success" is attitude. Let me say that number four on there is one I'd love to make number one. I'd love to say that the attitude of the store owner/operator is the most important thing in your business, but what our team found from our visits doesn't let me do that. No matter how good an attitude I have, I don't care how positive I am, if I don't have any money and I don't have any inventory, I will fail.

I can't argue with that, but I *can* tell you that time and time again, we saw the right attitude in the winning stores. The owners/operators get into a market, a competitive market, and the owners/operators are feeling good about what is happening in the business. They're tackling the problem, they're making decisions. You know, it works just like this: So goes the attitude of the store owner, so goes the attitude of the key management, so goes the attitude of the subordinate management, so goes the attitude of the employees, and that tells you exactly how they're going to treat the customers. You give me a store owner with a great attitude, and I'll give you a great store. Most of the time. Not always, but most of the time.

I visited a store in Brisbane, Australia, operated by a mate named Mike. The store is underneath a shopping center, of all places. I couldn't last ten days in that environment. It's not because I don't want to. It's that I wouldn't know how to get a customer to go down there. But Mike and his staff have figured it out. You walk into the store, and all you do is go, "There's such a great attitude." It took me no more than five minutes inside that store to feel the high energy.

And the only reason it could take five minutes inside the store is it might take that long to get oriented. At another store we visited in Australia, we started at the far left side of the store as you walk in, and we meandered through. When we got to the area where the computers are, they were doing their bidding on some of the storage stuff. There were people everywhere, and the rest of the store was empty. They might as well have had a barrier and shut the rest of the store down because everybody was right there at the computers. They were talking and interacting, having a good time. That's energy, man, and you can't buy that in business because it starts with the store owner of that business and it goes right down to the floor.

There's a huge hardware store in Colorado. No lumber/ timber for sale, no building materials, no insulation, no brick and block. But at the time I visited, they were doing $30 million a year in a store that's about 25,000 square feet. Now I'm standing in the main aisle with the store owner, and we're talking retail just as we all do, and the store owner is gazing out the window. We couldn't see the exact location where Home Depot was coming to town, about half a mile away, but he looked as if he actually could see it, and he said, "Art, Home Depot is going to come in here, and I'll be out of business in two years." I could not believe it. He wanted to walk away from a $30 million a year business because of Home Depot? They're good, but they're not that good.

We started talking about it. "What's the problem?" Here's what he said: "I no longer have the energy to fight." That's what the bottom line was in that scenario, and what he needed to do was develop a succession plan for his business. Take on a different attitude.

I'll tell you where I used to have a problem with that in my own family business. My son Eric has been in our business for as long as I can remember, and what I used to have trouble with was letting go of the financials, letting go of the bill paying, letting go of the P & L's at the end of the month and dissecting them. I just had trouble letting him take it over, even though he wanted to, and to be truthful, he was completely able to learn to do it fine.

Then because of my travel to consult with other retailers, one day I was working in the store and the next day I was gone, literally. Now he had to learn all this too quickly. It would have been so much easier and so much smarter on my part if I'd have just started taking time with him a few years before that to teach him, bring him up, bring him along. We've got to let it go by coaching and mentoring our staff. Keep the right attitude.

How can you expect a different result if you always do the same thing? Prepare your business for change.

# GOLDEN NUGGETS FOR NOW

- Keep in mind that the more money you make, the more time you have for your family and yourself.
- Remember that when kids coming up through the business don't see the parents' business allowing them to do what they like to do and have enough time for the family, the adult children won't want any part of it.
- Each day, strengthen your four top threads of success: Money, inventory, leadership, and attitude.
- Maintain the right business attitude. So goes the attitude of the store owner, so goes the attitude of the key management, so goes the attitude of the subordinate management, so goes the attitude of the employees, and that tells you exactly how they're going to treat the customers.
- Coach and mentor your staff.

# CHAPTER 4:
# ARE YOU AN AMATEUR
# OR A PROFESSIONAL?

*A thing is worth precisely what it can do for you, not
what you choose to pay for it.*
John Ruskin (1884)

In your business, mentor professionals, not amateurs. There are many too many amateurs in retailing. I want to tell you the differences between an amateur and a professional. As I go through these, you'll probably say to yourself, "Yes, I know one of those," or "There's somebody in my store like that." I don't care what position you have in the store, it doesn't matter to me if you're pushing a broom cleaning, I don't care if you're running a multi-billion dollar organization. You're an amateur or you're a professional, and some people have characteristics of both amateurs and professionals.

First off, with amateurs, the business runs you. All the amateur has done is buy themselves a job. If you spend all your day on the floor, who is running the store? You cannot run a business by spending all day, every day on the floor because you have no clue what is happening to the finances in your business when you do that. Let's say you don't go back to your store today. Let's say you don't go back to your store for three months. What happens to your business?

Think about that now, please, and if you say something like, "Well, if I'm gone, nobody will do the ordering," then your business is in big trouble. That's the way amateurs operate, and they're not really smart business operators. They're really self-employed because if you take them out of the business, the business has no value at all. Zero.

You want to be able to take somebody out of a business and have that business still have a value. Now with professionals, they work *on* the business, not just *in* the business.

Amateurs hope they make money, while professionals set bottom-line goals and they budget. Hope is a wonderful thought, but hope alone is not a strategy for success. If you told me you had a business strategy for you to make more money this year, here's what you would know: You would know how much money you made last year. You would know how much money you want to make this year. And number three, you would have an action plan with specific tactics to make that extra money. Bruce and I call this a MAP: A Management Action Plan.

There is going to be no need for hoping in that at all. That is a plan that is laid out. It is not overly detailed because I'm just like you. You give me a plan with a thousand different tactics, and I'll do nothing. You give me a plan with two, three, or four critical action points, I've got a fighting chance to make that happen. Professionals have bottom-line profit goals.

What is the biggest problem for owners/operators of small to midsize retail businesses? Nope, it's not the Big Boxes. Sure, Big Boxes are a problem, but here's the biggest one: Too many small business retailers are financially challenged. They do not spend any time working on their financials. When they take a hit in margins, they're not aware of it until it's too late. A lot of them don't take inventories, they don't know what their shrinkage is, their expense base is going up, and they're not taking the increases in their expense base and passing it on to the consumer, and they don't have a bottom-line profit goal, and they don't even know how to figure out what their bottom-line profit is.

Do you know why small business retailers do not budget? What we fear, we stay away from. No one ever took the time to train the small business owners on how to budget, and no one makes them budget, so because they are not educated and no one is asking them to budget , they just do not do it. My experience in working with thousands of small business operators is that only about 10% do any kind of budgeting.

Do you budget? Okay, you want a definition? Think about the end of last month in your business, as you were getting ready to go into this month. The week before you went into this month, did you sit down to look at what you wanted to happen? Coming into the new month, did you have a pretty good idea of how much your final gross margin was going to be? How much your expense base is? Did you subtract your expense base from your final gross margin to determine if you were going to make any money for the month?

Professionals do that. In fact, some professional retailers are fanatical about it. Home Depot, Lowe's, and the other Big Boxes are, and that's who you're up against.

# Which One Are You?

## Amateur
- Business runs you
- Hope you make money
- Know-it-all
- Makes excuses
- Blames others
- Someone else's problem
- Talks
- Individual
- Emotional decisions
- Dwells on the past
- Keeps their knowledge
- Everything is acceptable
- Energy vampire
- Follower

## Professional
- You run the business
- Set B.L.P. goal and budget
- Always learning
- Makes a difference
- Personal accountability
- Helps find solutions
- Executes
- Team member
- Business decisions
- Looks to the future
- Teaches others
- Sets high standards
- Always positive
- Leader

Amateurs know it all. Professionals are always learning. This is an absolute key ingredient. The fact that you're reading this book is evidence you are on your way to becoming a professional. You know that you know a lot, but you're smart enough to realize that you don't know everything. You're thinking that maybe there's a fighting chance that you're going to pick up a couple of nuggets from this book. You're going to take those nuggets, and you're going to run back to your store, and you're going to figure out how they're relevant to your business, and you're going to execute them and start making more money. And then you will start looking for the next nuggets.

Amateurs, they probably wouldn't make it even this far into the book. They'd say, "There is not anybody in this world who could teach me anything. I know everything there is to know about retail because I've been in retail for such a long time." The best, the most successful retailers in our industry, are lifelong learners. One example is Rich, a retailer I've known for many years. He takes an idea, a nugget, makes it relevant to his business, and executes. This concept has made Rich very successful.

Amateurs make excuses why things don't get done. Professionals make things happen. Never, ever call yourself a failure at anything you do until you blame somebody else for what went wrong. The second you blame somebody else, the second you do that, you can pat yourself on the back and call yourself a failure if you want to. Up until that point, all you're doing is trying new things, and there's nothing wrong with trying new things in your business. There's nothing wrong with it, and there's nothing wrong with being wrong. Every mistake in the world you can think of in retail, I promise you I've made it. I've lost a lot of money in this business, and I've made a lot of money in this business. I've made some really stupid mistakes along the way. It's because I just didn't know any better. Amateurs make excuses. Amateurs blame other people for what went wrong. Professionals understand personal accountability.

A story to show you what I mean: I'm sitting down with a couple of retailers in Chicago at dinnertime. The reason I'm sitting down with them is that they're very, very close to going out of business. The creditors are biting at the door. I'm there because they owe their vendors a lot of money, and the vendors are concerned they'll go belly up before they're able to pay. So I'm sitting there, and the woman just starts beating up their co-op about everything. Oh, they did this wrong, they did that wrong.

I'll tell you what. Honestly, I've got about fifteen seconds worth of patience for that. I carry around with me what's called a retailer two-by-four. So after those fifteen seconds, I take that retailer two-by-four and just go whack, right upside the lady's head. When she comes to, she says, "Why in heaven's name did you do that?" I answer, "Well, we've got about two hours. If you want to sit here and talk about everything that went wrong for those two hours, I'm going to get up and leave because that is totally unproductive, and my time is worth more than that. If you want to talk about how to learn for the future, where you are today, where you need to go, and how we get you there, and you want to make a difference in your business, I'm your man. Otherwise, I'm gone."

I'm not going to spend twenty seconds with somebody who wants to blame other people for what went wrong. It is absolutely nonproductive. Nobody wins from it, and all the retailers are who do that is what I call energy vampires. They suck the positive energy right out of you.

Professionals understand personal accountability. They say, "Hey, that's my store." In this case I'm telling you about, I asked the woman, "If your store goes bankrupt tomorrow, who is going to pay the bills for you?" She thought about it, and then answered, "Well, we're going to have to pay them." That's right. That's personal accountability. When you get up in the morning and look at the mirror, who's looking back at you? You are the one there. It's personal accountability. But for amateurs, it's always somebody else's problem.

Professionals, on the other hand, help find solutions. I run across that in our business all the time. Employees come to me wanting to dump problems on my shoulders. I don't know how you handle that, but I would never take an employee's problem unless it was only me who could fix it. And even then, all I would do is turn around and go, "What do we need to do to correct this problem? You know a lot more about it than I do." Then I expect the employee to give me a solution or help me find a solution. They'll only bring it to me one time without coming to me with a solution next time, and I expect them to do that. That's the way professionals operate because they are always involved in finding solutions.

Amateurs do a whole lot of talking. Professionals do a whole lot of executing. Retailers, and remember that I'm a retailer, like to talk. And talk some more. As you read this book, I'm sure you can tell that I love to talk and talk. I've a tremendous amount of respect for retailers who can talk about it and then do what they say they are going to do. There aren't a lot of retailers who can talk about it and then go do it. There are lots of retailers who can talk about it, but they can't execute. They don't know how to execute, and executing, implementing what's decided, is a very important part of being a professional.

If I walked into your store, the first place I'd go to so I could tell what your store will look like is the check stand area, and you could do the same if you walked into my store. Your check stand area is where you take care of your customers. I'd go right up to where your registers are. I guarantee you this: If that area is a mess, the rest of your store will be even worse. If the area is neat, clean, and organized, I can't guarantee the rest of your store will be that way, but it's a pretty good indicator. Why? Because the management in the store walks past the register area all day long. If it isn't important for them when they're walking past it, nothing else in the store is important enough either.

Next look at your signage, how you're using your signs and what the signs look like. Look at end caps, display, lights up in the ceiling, how clean the floors are. When I look at all those things, I know what the retailer's standards are. I know what's acceptable to them and not acceptable to them. I know what they can execute.

I attend a lot of meetings. On one occasion I listened to a retailer complaining like crazy about what Ace was not doing. I had the opportunity to visit this retailer's store the following week. Oh my gosh, what a mess the store was. No standards at all. This is a perfect example of an amateur retailer.

Then, if we put aside thinking about the in-stock position for a minute, the one thing that I can predict your success the most on comes when I get close enough to listen to your employees talking to your customers. That is how I'm going to learn about what your future success is. That's how I'm going to learn about it because I'm going to know whether you're coaching your people, I'm going to know whether they're trained, I'm going to know whether the customer is important to them or not.

A while back, I went into a large home center and headed towards the back of the store, walking down the main aisle. I can't find anybody who will say anything to me. So a young lady comes out. She looks at me, we make eye contact, and believe it or not, what she does is to walk right past me. When she's a little bit past me, I said, "Hi, how are you?" That's all I said. What did she say back? Nothing. Absolutely nothing. In fact, she completely ignored me. Completely. Now I have to tell you that it made me stop for a second to think to myself, "Am I offensive? Did I forget to take a shower for a few days?" These are not the kinds of things we want our customers thinking when they come into our stores. We must not ignore the customers, but that's what happens in too many retail businesses.

Why does that happen? One reason is that there are loads of amateur retail staff out there, and for amateurs, it's all about the individual. Professionals don't think that way. They understand the importance of a team. The team-work between the salesperson on the floor and the customer. Also, the teamwork among staff and the teamwork needed to make a  co-op strong. We have retailers out there who say, "Aw, we don't need you guys. We're doing just fine on our own." I say, "Who is going to negotiate all your pricing points for all your products, who's going to do this, who's going to do that?" Those retailers start getting the feeling that it's easier working with people than against them. Owners/operators see co-op staff as part of a team, retailers teaming up with each other.

Let's move on with contrasting amateurs with professionals: Amateurs make emotional decisions. Professionals make decisions based on what is best for the business. One small part of that: Suppose you're moving your store a quarter mile down the road. How many of your employees are you going to keep in your new location? Well, if you say anything less than 100%, then I've right off got a follow-up question: Why do you have them on the payroll now?

You know, it is okay to fire an employee. I love to use Sherry (not her real name) as an example. I kept Sherry for years past the date that she should have been gone. I understand the challenges here. I've gone through those challenges as well in getting employees who will do what needs to be done, but sometimes we just hold on to them too long. Sherry ran the tool department for a long time, but she was never going to advance anywhere in our business at all. I kept her and kept trying to work with her. One day Eric, my son, came to work, and he said, "I'm going to go down there and fire Sherry today." Hey, why didn't he do that three years earlier?

When Eric told me what he was doing, it took such a load off my mind. I was so emotionally attached that I just couldn't come to the decision. I felt like I had so much going on in running the business that I could not come to the decision to let her go. But we must make business decisions. We must make decisions based on what benefits the business, not just what feels comfortable to do. We must be able to make tough decisions. That's another sign of being a professional.

Amateurs dwell on the past. Professionals look to the future. A huge indicator. You've heard it plenty of times before. Learn from the past. I don't want to make the same mistakes twice, and I don't want you to make the same mistakes twice. I want to get better every day, and I want you to get better every day. But let's not spend energy dwelling on the past. Let's move on. It's done. Get over it. Where do we have to go? That's what matters. Focus on where we are going, not on where we have been. Where we've been was yesterday. Today I want to know what you've done for me today. Where are we going today?

I've worked with retailers where all they want to do is dwell on the past, and it's totally nonproductive. You have a limited amount of time, you have a limited amount of resources, let's put money attached to that, and you have a limited amount of energy. Now I don't know about you, but I'm big on using that energy correctly. I'm big on it because if you work with those retailers I call energy vampires, they'll suck every bit of energy out of your body in about thirty seconds. And then all you want to do is go find a bar and get filthy drunk. Instead of moving forward, after those experiences, we move backward. Why do people spend time living in the past? The past is known. They are more comfortable talking about what they know. Professionals move beyond this. Professionals are comfortable talking about the future.

Okay, back to the list of differences: Amateurs keep all their knowledge up in their heads. Professionals teach others. You have some very smart people working in your business and other businesses where you know the people. How many of the very smart people who really do understand the business are willing to stand up in front of the group and share the knowledge that they have? More important, since you're the one reading this book now: Are you willing to do that? There are retailers who say, "I learned the hard way, and I've been in this business like for a thousand years. The others need to learn the hard way, the same way I did." And even though they've been in retailing a long,

long time, they are still the amateurs. Let's all be professionals. Let's teach others what we know. Let's educate them, and then let's work with them together.

Another angle on this: A very smart Australian, John, gave me this nugget: If you've been in retailing for, let's say, twenty years, do you have twenty years worth of learning or do you have one year of learning repeated twenty times? Amateurs absolutely stop learning. They think that because they've been at it for twenty years that they've a vast amount of experience. When you start talking to them, though, you find out how limited their knowledge is. They really have one year of experience repeated twenty times.

Professionals show leadership in ways that energize. As I've said, amateurs are often energy vampires. Professionals are positive. Now, I'm all for constructive criticism. What did we do right, what did we do wrong, and what do we need to do to fix it? Let's go down the road and fix it. It does none of us any good if we fail to get the problems fixed.

Am I saying that professionals do not give input when something's wrong? No. You'll never see a professional sit back and let it happen, but when they come to the table, they'll come to the table with a clear statement of the problem, and they'll come to the table with some possible solutions for how the problem can be fixed. Amateurs follow, while professionals lead.

With amateurs, anything in the store is acceptable. On the other hand, professionals set high standards and do not accept inferior performance. It's just like this. A simple question: Do you want the employees in your store talking to your customers? At the Big Boxes, most times they don't. So do you want the employees in your store talking to your customers? I think you do. Okay, so do you allow your employees to greet your customers with a question that can be answered yes or no? More specifically, do you allow the people who work for you in your store to greet a customer with, "May I help you?" You see, about eight out of ten times, maybe nine out of ten, if a customer is asked, "May I help you?," they'll answer, "No."

Professionals train themselves and their employees to greet every customer with an open-ended question, one that encourages a little conversation between the employee and the customer. Questions like

"What do you have going on today?"

"What project are you working on today?"

"Which aisle can I take you to?"

"What product can I take you to?"

"How can I help you today?"

There are loads more standards that professionals set: How do you want the employees in your store to thank the customers who come in? How do you want to consistently sign end caps? Do you know that if you put up a sign on an end cap that has only the price and display the product down below, you increase your sales by 200% to 300%? But I've been in stores that don't have signs on the end caps. Those retailers are amateurs.

I know that not every store will have the same standards, and sometimes circumstances mean you bend a standard. Let's say your standard is, "Never point to another aisle. Walk the customer to the location of the product they've asked about." Okay, but now there are four different customers standing around wanting the attention of your one employee in that department on the sales floor, and she's gotten on her radio to call for backup help, but the help hasn't come yet, and a guy walks up to the one employee and says, "Where's the men's room?" Maybe it's okay to point instead of giving a personal escort. There are always exceptions. Deal with the exceptions and move on. The important part is that you think through really carefully what your standards are, and especially the ones that are nonnegotiable. Those are the standards where an employee says, "I don't want to do it that way," and you say, "Let's think about that one again until you get it right."

How do you want your employees to dress in your store? That's another standard. What do you want your employees to look like to the customer? Have you ever thought about it? Do you have a standard, a very specific way you want them to look? And I'd argue all day long, first of all a name badge is absolutely mandatory. I hope it is in your business. Do you let an employee out on your floor without a name badge? I hope you don't. If an employee comes to work without a name badge, they either have to get another name badge or maybe write their name on their forehead. When I said this in one workshop I was doing, a retailer named Mark raised his hand. I said, "Yes, what do you have, Mark?" He told all of us, "In our store if an employee doesn't have their badge, we give him a badge, but we also get him a set of Mickey Mouse ears, and he gets to wear those all day." I'm not sure I'd go that far. But come to think of it, I did tell you that having the employee write their name on their forehead was an option.

The name badge is the most important single item. Still, the dress code standard needs to go beyond the name badge. I was working with a retailer on the East Coast of the U.S. We were in the main aisle talking retail, and an employee walks by, with a customer following him. I knew the guy was an employee because he had his name badge on the front of his white T-shirt. He'd come right into the main aisle. I'm looking at him as he makes a turn, and I read the back of his T-shirt. It's the name of a rock band. The name includes two four-letter words I would not dare include in this book because they are so offensive.

This guy walks off into a side aisle with the customer still walking behind him with the back of that T-shirt in plain view. I look the store owner right in the eyes, and I say, "Is that your employee?" He turns his head to see the guy, who is now in the side aisle. The owner says, "Yes, that's Barry." I say, "How can you let him dress like that because I'm taken aback." The owner says, "Well, I guess that's because we don't really have any dress code."

Please do not let that happen in your store. Set a dress code. Set the other standards. This is what professional retailers do. The standards that you set in your store, and those standards that you execute, tell me more about you as an individual than anything else because then I know what you can get done, not what you just talk about getting done.

Of course, just setting the standard isn't enough. You must implement the standard. This means training staff, coaching staff, starting from the top down. A lot of people don't understand how to introduce a standard and make it stick in their business. We're all human beings, so think about how human beings learn. What we only hear, we often forget. What we see, we're more likely to remember. What we do, we understand, but only what we can teach others, can we master.

If you say, "Well, I told my staff what the standards are," I'd come back with, "Did you also give it to them in writing so they could go over it again later? Did you demonstrate to them how it's done, and then did you observe them doing it and give them constructive criticism? When they were ready, did you have them teach the standard to others? And throughout it all, did you encourage them to ask you questions about anything they didn't understand, and did you invite them to suggest improvements on the standards for you to consider? Did you look them in the eye and ask, 'Can you do that?'"

I go by a saying that is pretty simple: "If you don't train them, don't blame them."

Also, don't assume that one-time training is enough. It certainly isn't. Give refresher training, including asking each employee to recommit to the standard. Maybe you think employees will object to all this, but the truth is that employees, being people, are more comfortable at work when they know what's expected of them. Even for those employees who don't like the standards, the training, and the refresher training, doing this is a good business decision. That's what really counts, because you are up against the competition. You're a professional.

Training, coaching, and follow-up also are essential when it comes to systems, such as systems for handling money. Your computer system most likely prints off the amount of money that should be deposited into a bank every day, and then you check it against the bank deposits to make sure the money did get into the bank. So I'm thinking that you have an individual in your store who counts money and makes deposits. If the person doing that is you, the store owner/operator, that's fine with me. But if it's anybody else, you need a system, you need training, you need coaching, and you need follow-up.

Let's say you have somebody who comes in every day, goes into the office, opens up the safe, pulls out the drawers from the previous day, sits them down on the table, reconciles each one of the drawers back to $100 or $150 or whatever you have in the drawers on a regular basis, makes up a deposit, sits down at the computer, puts a little note in there on what the deposit is going to be, puts the money in a bag, puts it back in the safe, and goes about their day doing whatever they're going to do. Then at the end of the day, they get this bag, they put it in their pants or their pocket or whatever they do, they take it to the bank, and they sit down in front of the banker, who counts the money, signs the deposit slip, and gives it back to the employee, who goes home, knowing the bank's got the money. When that person comes back to work the following day, they go into the computer system and put the check mark next to the deposit, meaning it was all there, and they go about their day.

Whew, that's a system. But wait, there's more. At the end of the month, or shortly thereafter, you get an accounting of all your deposits and all your expenses, and the same person who did all of that stuff before is the same person as the one reconciling your checkbook.

Whoops. Now a good system has developed a bad problem. There are not at all enough checks and balances in that system. Recall that the job for Bruce Sanders and me in this book is to maximize your profitability, so with Bruce standing beside me, I want to warn you loud and clear: If you have a money handling system with a problem like I've just described, you are going to take a financial hit sooner or later that will dig into your profitability. It is just a matter of time.

Need convincing that it can happen to somebody like you? Okay. A father wants to phase out of his retail business, so he gives his son the responsibility of operations of the floor, including ordering. He says to his daughter, "You take care of the back office in the business. You do all the accounting, all the deposits, the human resources." Two years pass by, at which point, the son goes to his father to say, "Dad, could you put some more money into the business?" Dad says, "What do you mean?" "Well," says the son, "I've some bills to pay, and there's no money in the account." Dad says, "I haven't pumped money into this business for twenty five years." The son comes back with, "I don't know what to tell you, Dad, but we've got bills, and we've got no money."

Dad gets excited about it—no surprise there—and hires a forensic auditor. By the end of the audit, they discovered that for the past two years, the daughter has been embezzling money out of the business to the tune of $750,000. A hit to the bottom line of three-quarters of a million dollars.

Then it got even a little worse. The auditors saw that the daughter and her husband, who was in construction, had an account with the store, but hadn't paid on the account for the two years since Dad left the business. That added $10,000 to the damage.

I'm told that when the daughter was interviewed, here's exactly what she said: "Dad, all I was doing was getting my inheritance before you died." That's the way they think. Thieves are going to make excuses, so you must be careful. You must have systems in place that include safeguards, checks, and balances.

Dad and his son did not press charges against the thief. She was, after all, a close member of the family. I can only imagine how their next Thanksgiving gathering came off, though.

It's been hard for me to accept that family members would cheat each other like that, but I'm coming around.

A while back, I was working with a group of retailers and told them the story of the $750,000 loss. Then about six months later, I was doing training for what's called a group leader meeting. This is where Ace Hardware Corporation brings together all the group leaders from around the United States. We do some training for a couple of days on how to improve leadership skills.

After the meeting is finished, this older couple comes walking towards me. The gal is in tears. I say, "What's wrong Wendy?" She starts to answer, but then can't say anything, so her husband picks it up. "You know, Art, about six months ago, you were talking to the retailers in our area, and you talked about the possibility that someone might be taking money out of the back end of the store, out of the office, and we'd been having cash flow issues, and we didn't really understand it because our sales were actually pretty good. So we started looking at what you told us to look at. We started looking at, did the money that was supposed to get to the bank get to the bank? And we started seeing that every day it was off by just a little bit, $50 here, $100 there, $200 here, and anyway to make a long story short, in just a little period of time, this employee had pilfered about $75,000 out of the store."

Why was Wendy crying so hard? I think it was because the employee who did this is Wendy's sister. There are people out there, like Wendy, who take this kind of thing personally.

This is gut-wrenching stuff. It rips your heart out. These are people who are your best friends, family members, people you've brought up in the business. Please don't get me wrong. I'm not saying you distrust everybody. All I'm saying is to be aware and have systems in place.

When it comes to money, you'll want good systems for more than bank deposits. Here is another example. Great retailer. First class. Loses a back-office person, hires somebody, they get acclimated into the business, but little did the store owner know that the person they hired had started a plumbing company. Not a real plumbing company, but that didn't help much, given the flaws in the system. The company had a mailing address. What this guy was doing after about six months was creating invoices to the store. He was doing the check runs, he was the one who was cutting the checks, attaching the invoices to them, putting them in front of the store owner, and the store owner was signing them. The retailer was hit for well over $100,000.

Somebody has said that if you have ten people working for you, two people are never going to steal from you, no matter what. You could set the money right in front of them, and they'd take the money and say, "Here, boss, you dropped this money." There's no way they're going to steal from you. Two of them are going to try to steal from you no matter what you do. It doesn't matter. And the behavior of the other six will be based on opportunity. So we need systems in place to reduce the opportunities.

So think about this and decide what you want to do. Just another nugget for you to consider. If you decide to take action, go ahead to take action. You say, "Oh, man, Martha's been counting that money for a thousand years." No, it's okay if she counts the money. Just don't let her also reconcile the checkbook. So you say, "Okay, I'll start reconciling the checkbook, but how am I going to tell Martha?" That's simple. Honest people respect checks and balances. You go to Martha, and you say, "Hey, you know what? I'm going to start reconciling the checkbook. I want to get more involved in where this money is going." An honest Martha will respond, "Thank you. I have enough to do anyway."

If Martha replies, instead, "What's the matter. Don't you trust me?," I'll be thinking to myself, "No, not any more." That reply is a red flag you can run up a tall pole. If I told somebody in my back office that I was going to do that, and they said that to me, I would start auditing every single piece of paper they did because I am clearly thinking they may have been stealing from me for a long time, and I just don't know how they're doing it.

Shrinkage, as you probably know, is loss through employee theft, public theft, supplier theft, and bookkeeping errors. The average hardware store has 3% shrinkage. For a million-dollar business, that is $30,000 just disappearing. About 48% of shrinkage is internal theft, 32% is external theft, and the rest of it is miscellaneous paperwork or vendor shortages. When a retailer says to me, "No way this could happen in my business," all I say is, "Yea, right." I know better and personally have been burned several times by dishonest employees. If you think this is not happening to you, think again.

Fraudulent voids and refunds by cashiers could become an important cause of cash shrinkage. Our cashiers run about 8% of their transactions in a void or refund. We know that. It's roughly 8%. If the cashier gets to 16% or even gets over 10%, we've got a problem. Either they need training or they're stealing from us. We watch it, and we let them know we're watching.

Something you might not have thought about: Overages are worse than shortages. When thieves are stealing on the register, they're doing it a lot of times with fraudulent refunds, and they mentally try to keep track of their fraudulent refunds, but they can't. They're not smart enough to keep track of it, or maybe they're just too lazy, since they are thieves, after all. They do refunds for $50, but they only take $40 out of the register that day, so the register shows up as being $10 over. The store owner doesn't care if they're over, so the store owner doesn't say anything. If you have cashiers who have consistent overages in your store, you have a problem. It could be a training problem, but it also could be a ripping-off problem.

You even need systems for taking out the trash. If you've got anybody in your store who loves to take out trash like the Energizer Bunny and they're looking at the clock and it's a quarter to 6:00 and they work until 6:00, and they say, "Boss, can I start taking out the trash yet?," well, watch out.

Let's say you're not watching out carefully enough, so you say yes, and this employee runs around the store really fast. What you don't see for a number of nights, though, is he's got the trash, and he runs past the hardware department and throws a power tool in and runs by the tool department and throws a hammer in there, and he runs outside and tosses it all in the trash.

Two hours after he leaves the building, you go back and stand out there and see the guy come back to the trash. "Say, Alex, what are you doing?" "I don't know, boss, I just found all this stuff in the trash."

If you let that back door open with nobody around it, I'll tell you what. There are a whole bunch of horror stories out there. I don't need to tell you about the time when the guy runs out the back door, and what a coincidence, his buddy is driving by at the same time, and an even bigger coincidence, the window is open in the car, so the guy tosses whatever in the back of the car and runs right back inside.

A high percentage of all businesses that fail in the first five years in the United States fail because of shrinkage. They don't realize it until it's too late, and then they don't have any money to back it up. The money is all gone. It just disappeared out of the business. All I'm saying is be careful and look out. After hearing all the stories from other retailers, I've gotten careful and I look out. But I still can be fooled:

It's the middle of the night, and I am asleep. The phone rings. It's a call from the police department asking me to drive down to the store. When I arrive, I see police officer Rick. I know Rick. He comes into my store regularly. I say, "Hi, Rick, what's happening?" He says, "Take a look inside the back of my patrol car." "What do you mean?" "We caught two guys in your store. Take a look at them in the back of my patrol car." I say, "No, man, I don't need to do that. Just take them to jail and throw away the key." Rick, like any good police officer, doesn't let up, and in fact gets more insistent. "Art, come with me and look inside my patrol car." I walk over. Rick is standing by the back of the car, shining his flashlight through the rear window. I stare in.

I'll be honest with you. When I saw what was inside, my very first thought was, "What the heck is John, my warehouse manager, doing in there sitting next to the thief?"

# GOLDEN NUGGETS FOR NOW

- Develop your MAP to success, your Management Action Plan.
- Avoid energy vampires and certainly never be an energy vampire yourself.
- Frequently walk past your store's cash register area to be sure it is neat, clean, and organized.
- Regularly ask yourself which employees you would not keep if you moved your store to a new location, and then question why you have those employees on the payroll now.
- Learn from the past, but think and talk about the future.
- Each year you work on your business, be sure that you are gaining one year more of learning, not just another year of the same lessons.
- Train yourself and your employees to greet every customer with an open-ended question.
- On each end cap, put up a sign that has only the price, and display the product down below.
- Be sure every employee wears a name badge.
- To make a standard stick, tell it, put it in writing, demonstrate it, observe employees doing it, and have employees teach it to others.
- Always keep your employees in the know about just what you expect of them.
- Keep checks and balances in your money handling systems.
- Look very carefully at what's really happening if you see a cashier with consistent overages.
- Sign your store as if you have no sales people, and train your staff as if you have no signs.
- Set high standards and do not accept inferior performance.

# CHAPTER 5:
# WHAT MAKES YOUR
# BUSINESS WORLD-CLASS?

*It doesn't help to remember the price of*
*yesterday's roast beef.*
Ben Johnson (1637)

What specifically do you do in your business that's going to boost your success and maximize the chances your business will still be operating three years from now? You've got to be absolutely world-class at something. Otherwise, some competitor will come in to rip market share away from you. Before you know it, your business is gone from the face of the earth.

Think of it in terms of what's called an elevator speech. Let's say that as you're waiting for an elevator, the person you're standing with asks, "Why should I shop at your store?" And then the elevator doors open, you and the other person get in, and you've got about thirty seconds, while the elevator is moving, to answer the question. What do you say? Keep it focused because you don't have much time.

Okay, now I'll give you more time than thirty seconds, but in exchange, I'll make the question a little more complicated: What are the top ten reasons for somebody to shop at your store? See, you really need to have multiple differentiators. It will start with your staff being better, your customer service dazzling the customer, but don't let your people be your only differentiator. The more competition that comes into your market area and the tougher the competition gets, the better it is to have multiple differentiators.

> **Which one (or more) are you?**
>
> 1. The biggest
> 2. The least expensive
> 3. The most distinctive
> 4. The best at customer service

You must be the biggest, the least expensive, the most distinctive, or the best at customer service. It is even better if you're more than one. Being the biggest deals with ranging or assortment. That's hard for the small to mid-size retail business. When you aim to be the least expensive, it is all about price. When you're on the cutting edge of price, it's easy to get sliced alive by a Big Box. So do you want to be the most distinctive? That means having a niche, stocking items or product lines that the competition does not carry, at least as completely as your store carries it. Or do you want to be the very best at customer service? That's where I think you probably want to be.

Whatever you decide on, you must execute. But the start is making the decision. The number one thing that prevents retailers from doing something is that they put off making a decision to do it. Then when it comes time to execute, remember how those amateurs think and behave. They just keep making all kinds of excuses as to why they can't get it done.

Also, there's the wait-and-see retailer. I'll get a telephone call from a retailer who tells me, "Art, I've got a new Home Depot coming in across the street from me." I say, "When are they going to open?" The retailer says "In four weeks" I say, "Well, what are you doing to get ready for them?" Maybe the answer is something like, "You know, my grandpa had this business a hundred years ago, my dad had it fifty years ago, and what I'm doing now worked for them. It's certainly going to work for me." Well probably not, because did your grandpa or your dad ever have a Home Depot come in across the street from them? For sure, the location of your business is important. When a Big Box moves into what we call the cutoff position, between the customers and your store, that can be a huge problem.

Some of those retailers get really stubborn at about this point, when I constructively criticize their approach. Hey, having pride in your business and loyalty to traditions isn't all bad, but you are not going to succeed if you get headstrong when change is forcing itself on you. We, as retailers, struggle with knowing exactly what needs to be changed. I think we talk about it, but we don't narrow it to exactly what tactics are required. We don't ask ourselves and the people on our teams what we need to do. Instead of just talking about it, actually do it!

You can't wait and see. If you haven't experienced it, you don't know what a Big Box can do to the small to mid-size retail business and how quickly they'll do it. Let me be really clear about this. Do not wait for another Big Box to come into your market to do anything. They're coming. It's just a matter of time. Run your business as if your most challenging competitor is going to move in across the street from you.

At a time when I had twenty-three Big Boxes within ten miles of my family's store, American River Ace Hardware, I found out that a Wal-Mart was opening up right around the corner. Some people said I didn't need to worry, since Wal-Mart doesn't carry a lot of hardware. But the truth is that Wal-Mart carries a fair amount of hardware, including a lot of lawn and garden products, and they are one tough competitor. If a retailer says to me, I'm going to kind of wait and see what happens, I get more than a little nervous because I know what Big Box competition can do to a retailer.

Differentiate your business. "Me too" stores are failing all over. Even what seem like small distinctions can make a big difference. I'll give you a little example in our market: Home

Depot and Lowe's do not carry open stock sandpaper. The other thing that I know is that they don't carry anything above a 600 grit. If you're doing any kind of refinishing at all on any kind of metal, you're going to use at least a 1000 or 1200 grit sandpaper. You're not going to spray paint over 600 grit. So you start to learn little things. They don't carry a complete selection of sockets, wrenches, taps and dies, or numbered drill bits. I make sure that my store carries those. It gives us confidence, for one thing, but the other thing that it does is it gives us an opportunity to make some money.

Another distinction is with the niche items. What products or product categories do you carry that the Big Boxes don't? Again, I'll give you an example from my family's store. We have an incredibly complete collection of fasteners. It is a world-class product assortment of fasteners. It's much broader than what is carried by any of the Big Boxes, or any of the other stores, for that matter, in my market area. People drive from 25 miles or more if they are, for instance, working on restoring a classic automobile, since we're the place they think of that is sure to carry the exact fasteners they will want. And by the way, while they're in the store, they'll catch up on their other shopping needs as well, so a niche will also expand your market. The niche will bring customers into our store who would have normally gone to another retailer.

Don't have some world-class distinction, and you're going to struggle. Do it right, and you deserve to have confidence. Being distinctive in your market can easily be the difference between success and failure.

There was a retailer in Colorado. He was devastated. Now here's a definition of "devastated" for you in the retailer's world. If a retailer is devastated, they're losing sleep at night because there's a new competitor coming.

I get into town with Frank, another retailing consultant, and we drive over to meet with the retailer, whose name is Mike. Next, the three of us get into the car to drive down the block to the brand new Lowe's. We're doing this because

Mike told us he thinks that Lowe's is going to put him out of business.

I know that Mike, who is looking pretty devastated right now, is one great retailer. He does a lot of things very, very well. As we're driving the short distance, I'm thinking that Mike's store is going to take a hit from Lowe's, but Lowe's isn't going to put him out of business. I'm thinking that Mike is too good a retailer for that to happen. I'm thinking that I want to be ready to build Mike's confidence when we visit Lowe's.

The three of us get out of the car, and we walk into Lowe's. As we walk in, I see that the first 96 feet of the store is nuts, bolts, and other fasteners. The entire floor layout of a Lowe's store is done for a reason. They've thought it through, and the store they open today is better than the store they opened yesterday because they evaluate those openings closely.

We walk right up into the fastener area. While we're standing there, a gentleman from Lowe's comes around the corner. I see from his name tag that he's David. He greets us with a great smile and asks what's going on. Then he notices that we have on Ace shirts. He asks, "Are you guys from the Ace store right down the block?" I say we are and introduce myself and Frank and then Mike as the store owner.

David, with that great smile, reaches out to shake hands with Mike and says, "I love your store." And Mike, who had been looking pretty tense, starts to smile himself. Frank, who was thinking a little bit quicker than either Mike or me, says to David, "What do you like about Mike's store?" David looks over at Frank and answers, "You wouldn't believe all the stuff he's got that we don't carry." Frank says, "Like what?" And now, with my objective of building Mike's confidence, it was like I'd gone into the store, looked up at David, gave him $1,000, and said, "Here, memorize this list, and then recite it when Mike comes in later." David from Lowe's starts naming all the fasteners, all the cabinet hardware, all the builders hardware, and he starts talking about all the little pull-out drawers, and he says, "I've been sending probably twenty people a day over to your Ace store for the last three weeks since we've opened."

I'll bet you won't be surprised to know that Mike, Frank, and I didn't even need to go through the rest of the store because my chief objective was to build the confidence of the store owner to know that he's going to compete just fine. He discovered the success factor: His store was distinctive.

Of course, walking through the rest of the store would be an excellent activity for Mike, or for any other retailer competing with Lowe's. You can always learn a lot from walking around the competition. When I ask retailers in small to midsize businesses why they don't visit the competition more regularly, they usually answer something like, "Gee, I just don't have the time in my schedule." Well, okay, that has some truth to it, but if I push it further, the answer underneath is often, "I'm afraid I'll see my customers there."

Actually, you may not see too many of your customers there, and that can build your confidence, too. Consider what happened to me at a store in a small community in California. The store is owned by a father and daughter. They run the business. At the time I visited, a new Home Depot had come in. There are not that many people in the whole community, but the father and daughter had done well there.

Now the three of us are going into Home Depot for the same sort of reason we went into the Lowe's in Denver. We're walking around the store, and we get to the paint department. The only thing I plan to do is ask the person at the paint department, "Do you carry Duckback Stain?" I know for a fact that they don't carry it, and I know Duckback Stain is very popular in this area. I'm thinking that the person at the paint counter will say no, at which point, I'll ask him where I could get it. If he says, "Ace Hardware," I'll thank him. If he doesn't, I'll tell him why I asked and say that if people want the product, he could direct them to the father and daughter's store.

We get to the counter. I'm with the father and daughter. We are standing there watching the salesman on his cell phone. We hear him trying to set up a date for that night. I finally get his attention and mouth the words, "I need to talk to you." But that doesn't make one bit of difference to this guy. He's still on his cell phone yakking away about getting a date.

No, he doesn't stop talking. Believe it or not, instead of that, he turns his back on us. I am now looking at the salesman's butt. I didn't want to have that in eyeshot for very long, so I turn to the daughter and say, "Would you let that happen in your store?" She answers, "Not in a million years, I wouldn't let that happen." I said, "Well, this is another reason why you're going to be fine, and these guys are going to be less successful because of you."

There is no doubt that you and I and other retailers like us can compete against the Big Boxes. The key is to understand what their strengths and weakness are, understand our own strengths and weaknesses, and then develop a plan to compete.

## GOLDEN NUGGETS FOR NOW

- Always know which one (or more) you are: The biggest, the least expensive, the most distinctive, the best at customer service.
- Run your business as if your most challenging competitor is going to move in across the street from you.
- Continue to put into action a range of ways to be distinctive in your market.
- Walk around the competition's stores, ready to learn.

# CHAPTER 6:
# YOUR RETAIL OPERATING PLAN

*There is no such thing as cheapness in the universe.
Everything costs its own cost, and one of our best virtues is
a just desire to pay it.*
John Ruskin (1884)

There are nine elements essential for retailing success. I've told you about some of them in previous chapters, and I'll talk about others later. But I want to list them all here with brief descriptions so you get the idea of how they can operate together to boost your profitability.

1. *Retail Operating Plan*. The financial numbers in a business are the single most important indicator of future success.
2. *Leadership*. This includes developing a company strategy, understanding what's important to an employee, and knowing where to spend your time. My research shows that your leadership ability as an owner/operator can impact the sales of your store plus or minus 15%.
3. *Technology*. Use your computer system as more than just an expensive cash register. Discover all the ways it can improve your profitability. Track receivables, payables, inventory productivity, and staff productivity. Later, I'll be describing how technology can help you out

tremendously as you work with your Retail Operating Plan, the element I listed above. Hey, I told you all the nine elements work together.

4. *Systems.* What I mean by this is that you must maintain systems for the consistent execution of procedures in your business. That goes from receiving and warehousing inventory up through processing the customer sale. You'll have systems for servicing the customer, to be sure customer needs are being met, and systems for handling the money, to be sure your employees aren't ripping you off. I hope you're not reinventing the wheel all the time. If you're handling cash in thirty different ways in your business, figure out the best way, make that the system, and start putting more energy into driving sales. Systems are also valuable for the multi-store owner. When you move staff between stores, life is much easier then.

5. *People.* Recruiting, selecting, hiring, training, disciplining, and firing staff. And with these and the rest of the human resource management functions, always remembering that the real bosses are the customers. Our people have to dazzle the customers. They must be available, willing, friendly and knowledgeable.

6. *Product Selection.* Okay, now stop a minute in the middle of the list here so I can ask you a very important question: What about your product selection makes a customer shop in your store and in any one of your departments? What makes you special? I told you how in my family's store, people come from miles around to find the fasteners they need. What is going to make customers come to your store from miles around for the product selection? Know who your customers are and what they expect from your product selection.

7. *Services.* What services, such as home delivery or gift wrapping, will you do that the competition cannot or will not do? But, you know, just having the services isn't enough. How do you train your staff and continue to coach your staff on telling customers about the services and in providing those services in world-class ways? Sometime soon, make a list of every service you do in

your business. And when was the last time you looked at what you were charging for your services? Make a conscious decision on what services you will charge for and which ones will be free and then SHOUT IT OUT to your customers. You might be surprised how many service you actually do.

8. *Standards.* I've already discussed this one when I pointed out the differences between an amateur and a professional. Here is where it fits in with the other eight essential elements. What are the standards in your business, the ones that employees know are nonnegotiable? What is so important to you in your business that if I came and worked for you, unless I did this, I would be fired?

9. *Top-of-Mind Awareness.* This covers branding, which I use to mean publicizing who you are and what you are world-class at doing. It covers customer relationship marketing, where you always know who your customers and potential customers are and market directly to them. This is a targeted, not shotgun, approach. And it covers advertising, where the small to midsize retailer usually delivers a message through tabloids, television or radio to attract customers.

All these nine together form what we call the Retail Pyramid of Profit. We've arranged the nine essentials in a pyramid for a reason. The Retail Operating Plan and the three just above it in the RPOP (Leadership, Technology, and Systems) are the most fundamental. You must have those in place before you move further. The five elements above (People, Product Selection, Standards, Services, and Top-of-Mind Awareness) will be what distinguishes you from the competition, what allows you to get the business that the competition is not getting. This is where you must be better than your competition.

I know that we left out what could possibly be the most basic element of all for retail success—location. We left it out intentionally. We figure that you have your location, so I want to work with you from there. I don't want to take a chance on wasting your time with something you can't do anything about for right now. And I do know there may be circumstances where a change in location will be your only choice.

I do want to pay lots of attention to the Retail Operating Plan. It consists of the financial numbers. The ROP is like the dirt, the soil, in your business. It is where your business springs from. Success, failure, the limits on your success, and the protections against your failure are all directly related to the numbers in your business. When you're building your business, what you need to be able to do is make sure that the numbers work.

What are the most crucial numbers in your business? I'd say that the top one is sales. Number two, in my opinion, is your final gross margin. Next is your expense base. For every dollar that comes through your cash registers, how much of that dollar is going to expenses? Number four, arguably, is inventory turnover, how fast you're turning the inventory in your store. Number five is cash flow. I know there are some retailers who would say cash flow is number one on the list of crucial numbers. I put it at five because cash flow is too short-term, in my opinion. But in any case, the cash flow of your business is right up there as a measure to consider. Next is obsolete inventory. How much dead stock are you carrying in your store?

The last of the crucial numbers I want to include in this top-importance list is your bottom-line profit. That is, how much money are you making? For every dollar that goes through your cash registers, how much of that dollar is profit to you?

I'm going to ask you another favor right now. In the margin of this page, please write down that number. For every dollar that goes through the front registers, how much of this dollar is profit you could reinvest in your company? If you don't know, guess. I'm talking annual average. I understand very clearly that it fluctuates by the month. At American River Ace, we lose a lot of money each January. Then in springtime, late March, we start to pick it all back up.

When you are done writing down that number, whether it was a guess or not, here's another one where you might need to guess. If you asked your hourly employees to write down that number, what would they write? In my experience, they'll write down some number between 30% and 50%. They really think that for every $100 that goes through the registers, you are keeping $30 to $50 in profit. I'm not criticizing them. I'm just saying that, based on my experience, many of your hourly employees, as well as some managers, simply don't understand your business.

I believe it is very important for the employees who work for us to understand that the store owners do not start campfires with $100 bills. Now if by chance you do start campfires with $100 bills, I not only apologize for making a bad assumption, but I also say good for you. I'll tell you that I use cheap kindling to start my campfires.

The reason that the employees come up with the 30% to 50% in profit is that they forget about the largest investment of all. It's inventory replenishment. I tell them, "We sold it. We've got to buy more." About 50¢ of every dollar I take in at the register goes to restocking inventory. And my business needs to pay that bill. Every other week, I get an invoice from Ace, and they have absolutely no sense of humor if we don't pay it. Now, I've got it figured out. I know if cost of goods was zero, we could make a lot of money in our business. But that's not how it works.

The other thing that hourly employees usually don't recognize is that it does *not* cost millions and millions of dollars to get into a retail business. It is not all that hard getting into the retail business. The really difficult part is making money in the business year after year. I am clear with my hourly employees, and my managers, for that matter, that I am not spending or making 50¢ on every dollar. I suggest you do the same, so that's another nugget for you to consider. Train your staff on how a dollar received through your registers is spent by the store.

The Retail Operating Plan will tell you how accurate you were in the number you wrote down in the margin of the page, and then you've a tool for educating you staff.

The ROP tells me there are only two numbers in your business that I need in order to know pretty much everything about your financial success or struggles with your business. You give me those two numbers, and also show me your cash flow statement, and I'll tell you where your problems are. First, I want to know your final gross margin. That is the percentage margin on your profit for the products in your store, with you subtracting the costs of markdowns, freight, all other transportation costs, taxes if applicable, and shrinkage. Then I want to know your expense base. That is the percentage of your sales that goes to pay for your payroll, occupancy, and all other expenses. This does not include amortization, depreciation, or payback on most principal debt. The only place you'll see payback on principal debt on financial statements is on the cash flow statement, so that's where I want to look at it. The retailer thinks they're making money, but they've got no money. The money they thought they should have is going to pay back mostly long-term debt.

What I hear from retailers is, "Art, our sales are about the same as they were last year. I don't know where the money is going." I say, "Well, I don't know where the money is going either, but I'll tell you what. In about half an hour we can find out where the money is going because I'm going to look at your margins, I'm going to look at your expense base, and I'm going to look at your cash flow statement. With those three, I'll see pretty much everything I need to know about the business."

It is not really that complicated. You take your final gross margin, after all markdowns, freight, and shrinkage. You subtract your expense base (payroll, occupancy, and all other). This is your bottom-line profit before taxes. So let's say your final gross margin is 40% and your expense base is 40% or 40¢ on every dollar the store is making. How much money are you making? That's right. Zero. Nothing.

If your expense base is higher than your final gross margin, when you do the math, write down the result with a red pen. That's because you're losing money. I have lost track of the number of retailers I've worked with who are what I call "upside down." That means your expense base is more than your final gross margin. When a retailer is upside down, they are using money they should be spending on inventory replenishment to pay expenses. This is the retailer whirlpool of death. The retailer is going out of business a little bit every day, and they do not even know what is happening to them.

So what can you do if you find yourself upside down in a hole? There are only four ways to bring you out and get you right side up. The first way is to drive sales while you leave margins and expenses the same. The second way is to leave sales and expenses where they are while you tweak margins up. Number three, leave sales and margins where they are and reduce expenses. And the last way is to drive sales up, tweak margins up, and reduce expenses, a combination of the three other ways. I'll tell you that for every single retailer I've ever worked with in my career who was upside down, the only way they came out of the hole was with that fourth method, the combination method.

As I say, the combination method includes tweaking margins upwards. When I talk about the owner/operator of the small to midsize business doing that, please understand how I suggest you go about it. I'll start out by talking about Lowe's again. Last time I checked, the final gross margin at Lowe's, a $50 billion company, was about 33%. Seven years before, the final gross margin at Lowe's was 27%, and the final gross margin at Home Depot was 29%. Over seven years, both of those companies more than doubled their sales and put anywhere from 4 to 6 additional margin points to the bottom line.

These are smart retailers. They did not get where they are by setting a similar margin for whole classes of merchandise. Consider my family's store, where Class 100 is floor care chemicals. Lowe's and Home Depot carry floor care chemicals, and they have different margins on different items in that class. This is called variable pricing, or as I call it, smart pricing. It consists of reviewing your entire assortment of products to set intelligent prices in order to achieve your bottom-line profit. So we need to do the same. We drill down as far as we reasonably can toward item pricing. We drill down into a classification of merchandise. We dissect it down to every single item in the class. Some items will carry a low margin, while other items will carry a high margin. That is how we maximize the profitability in our business. We are fortunate at Ace Hardware Corporation to have a very smart category management team. We use the retail pricing intelligence brought to us by the corporate office, plus a margin management tool which I'll tell you about later, and our own local knowledge to help maximize our profitability.

If you are still setting margins by overall product class, I'm going to think that you are not hurting enough for money. You are making too much money, and you're taking the easy way out by setting class margins. I would never set a class margin in all my life because that's not the way to maximize profitability. You go into the class and dissect the class. You look at it item by item, and you set margins based on what the market will bear. Some items within a class may be at 50–60% margin, while some items within that same product class are at 20–30%. One of the reasons to drill down towards the item level is to see what the margins actually are. I find retailers to have hundreds of products below a margin they would say is acceptable, and they just did not know it.

I'm a retailer and I know retailers, so I'm aware why we set class margins instead of drilling down towards the level of item pricing. We do it because it is quick and easy, and we're all pushed for time. But if I'd set margins by product classes, I would have been out of business a long time ago. We carry about 28,000 SKUs in our store, that is, 28,000 different types of items. Home Depot and Lowe's each carry about 50,000 SKUs in each of their stores. I consider myself very fortunate to have all those 28,000 SKUs because it gives me lots of approaches to get the additional margin points. We'll dig into those 28,000 SKUs and see where we can make our money. Smart retail pricing is knowing where in your assortment of products you need to go to make the money you need to be successful and, in our case, maintain an image in the market that our prices are fair. We will never be the price leader in our market.

Can I make a whole lot of money on Scott's Summerizer Fertilizer? No, I may not make even one dollar a bag. Home Depot and Lowe's have driven that market down to nothing. No profitability at all. They can do it. So I'm going to be right where I need to be on Scott's Summerizer Fertilizer in order to maintain my price image and get the customers coming in. We carry the item because customers expect that they can buy it from us.

And if Home Depot puts that item on the front page of their advertising circular, I can pretty much promise you that if we put that item on the front page of our ad, we're going to be right where Home Depot is at. We're going to be right where we need to be. When I was in Australia, I saw what Bunning's, which is a Big Box there, does with the ads of the smaller-sized competitors. They put those ads in the window right in front of the store with the competitors' prices on them right next to the Bunning's prices. So imagine that your store is up against Bunning's, and you go to visit them, as you should do with every competitor, and as you approach the store, there's a beautifully clean glass window with your latest ad posted right there, and then on the items they carry that you carry, they've got their lower prices.

There is only one reason to advertise. It's to drive customers into your store. If you are expecting to make a whole bunch of money on your ads, think again. If you look at our front page, back page, and pages four and five of our eight-page advertising circulars, many times we'll be at only 10% margin, and sometimes we'll be less than that. What we're aiming to do is to get those customers to come into our store, and when they come inside the store, that is where we've the opportunity to make some money.

But don't think for a minute that for every item we're advertising that Home Depot and Lowe's don't have, we'll forget to make money on sales of that item. Our memory and concentration aren't *that* bad. We are going to make money on those distinctive items. This will also help drive customers into our stores.

So we want to end up with managing margins as close as possible to the item level. That is the secret ingredient for improving your profitability. But remember that the Retail Pyramid of Profit shows us how all the nine elements work together. For the Retail Operating Plan, at the ground level, we want to look at what I call Dashboard Indicators.

What are your daily Dashboard Indicators? What numbers do you want to check on for every day you do business? Store sales, I hope. Overall store margins, I hope. Average transaction and voids by cashier, I hope. Maybe the weather, since when you put it together with sales figures, you can get a better idea of how to order inventory in the future. For the same sort of reason, knowing what advertising you had out on the street can be helpful with future decisions.

What do you want to check on every single week? How about payroll, sales by department, margins by department? How about your monthly Dashboard Indicators? Maybe inventory turnover, markdowns, and open to buy versus budget.

I call them Dashboard Indicators because, for me, your store is a vehicle, just like your car. It can take you wherever you want to go. But think about what you need to make that car do its job. Well, you need the key to start it up. Without the key, it's not going anywhere. For the store, it's money. I don't care what kind of store you have. If you don't have any money, you're not going anywhere. Then you need fuel, and that's why you have a gas gauge on your car's dashboard. The fuel for your business is your margins. If your margins start to slip and go down so you are operating upside down, the store that is your vehicle is not going to go very far. With each mile, it dies slowly. Or maybe not so slowly. In your car, you have other critical dashboard indicators like oil level, radiator temperature, tire pressure, etc. You also need to be aware of these critical dashboard indicators in your business, like payroll, open to buy, etc.

When I talk about margin, I really should say *margins* because there are four different margins to look at. They are called Sitting Margin, Front Door Margin, Back Door Margin, and Final Gross Margin. Stay with me here. It is not really that complicated. Here's how it works:

Let's start with Sitting Margin. If I took a snapshot of your current costs and retails right now, today, it would consider all of your sales on each item for the last twelve months on each of those SKUs. If you sold every item as you did last year, based on your current cost and retails, this is your Sitting Margin. It's a snapshot of your business at any given time. This number will give you indicators of when your margins are slipping.

| | | |
|---|---|---|
| Backdoor Margin | | 52% |
| Markdowns | 3% | |
| Freight | 2% | |
| Shrinkage | 3% | |
| Mrkdwns+Freight+Shrkge | 8% | |
| Final Gross Margin | | 44% |
| Payroll | 20% | |
| Occupancy | 7% | |
| All Other | 11% | |
| Total Expense Base | 38% | |
| Bottom-Line Profit (pre-tax) | | 6% |

Back Door Margin is how much you pay for the product and what your current retails are when it comes off the truck. Some retailers will include any value-added taxes, tariffs, transportation costs, and duties in the cost of goods, since they are a part of what you pay for the product. Some retailers will have freight as a line item on their Profit & Loss Statement. Most international retailers include all costs to get a product to their back door in their cost of goods. I don't include those there in figuring Back Door Margin. I take care of the freight costs when I calculate Final Gross Margin. But however you do it is fine with me as long as you include all costs of getting a product to your back door somewhere in the calculations.

To get Front Door Margin, subtract from the Back Door Margin the margin impact of sales due to markdowns. This includes any way that you mark down products: Employee discounts, sale discounts, contractor discounts, liquidation or inventory reduction discounts, best friend discounts, best enemy discounts, family discounts.

Do you know the impact on your margins all of your markdowns have? Most retailers that I work with don't monitor that number at all. They have no idea. No clue. I can tell you what it is in an average store. In an average store, the margins are impacted by 2 to 3 margin points because of markdowns. For my store, it's about 6 MP instead of 2 MP to 3 MP. It is so much more because we do a lot of advertising in Sacramento. In the retailer group I told you about earlier, we budget a lot of money to entice customers into our stores by doing a tremendous amount of advertising. We do 24 tabloids a year, and we do at least six events a year, we do some radio, we do some television. We do a lot of loyalty marketing. Loyalty marketing gives discounts and rewards to customers who join our Ace loyalty rewards program. All of this is part of an annual plan. We're not spending money on advertising just to see how much we can spend. We know exactly what we're branding, marketing, and advertising every month. This is a very detailed, well thought out plan. If you don't have a plan like that, I strongly recommend you develop one.

I said we do at least six events a year. Actually, six is a barebones minimum. Events are huge for us. In the mid-1990's, when we would put out an advertising tabloid, our sales would spike just like that. We could depend on it. Today, when we drop a tabloid, we don't get anywhere near as big a spike as we used to get. We are not going to stop doing tabloids. Doing them is a great way to keep the top-of-mind awareness out there and it's a great way to get new customers. Still, we can't put all of our marbles into the tabloid basket anymore. So we funnel some of those dollars into loyalty club marketing, we funnel some of them into branding, we funnel some of them into radio and television to give us a complete program. We don't have any choice. That's why our markdowns are so high as a percentage of our sales. As long as we know what impact the markdowns are going to have, we can budget for this.

With events, I'm big into champions. I'm big into holding people accountable. Whenever we schedule an event, there is going to be an individual, one person, responsible for executing that event in our store. They own that event. Over time, we learn who the winners are, the great employees who show leadership and initiative. We all should have more champions taking care of different areas in running the store.

Another successful way to get customers back into our store is with bounce-back coupons. We're not the first retailers to use them. In fact, we're not the first retailers to do anything. We're waiting for somebody else to be successful with it, and then we'll use it. With a bounce-back coupon, we want to get our customer back in the store again in the near future. For instance, if this week we're advertising and we've got an eight-page tab, but the following Saturday we've got nothing, we may use a bounce-back coupon during the ad period to get the customer to come back in our store on the following Saturday.

A bounce-back coupon that works very well for us is 50% off any single item that retails for under $30. Now think about what I'm suggesting here. How much would you pay a customer to walk every single aisle of your store? Think about the customer who comes into your store, goes right to a specific aisle, picks up exactly what they came in for, and leaves without any real idea of everything else you stock. The bounce-back coupon gets your customers walking up and down most aisles in your store looking at your product selection because they're trying to figure out how they're going to use their 50% discount. We find that about seven out of every ten of those customers with the coupon also buy something else, and at the margins we're carrying, we're really not losing any money on this. The fact is we're getting more customers in, so we're increasing sales right then and we're building knowledge in the customers of all the different things we can sell them. As I write this, we are planning to do a 50% off any single item that retails under $50.00 next year as an event for our retailer group. What do you think of that idea?

We use the bounce-back coupons about four times a year because we think you can wear it out. But do the math. If you take your customer base and you could get every customer who comes into your store to come back into your store one more time during the year, just one more time, you might put a competitor out of business. What you do is multiply the number of transactions based on the best customers you've got in your store times your average transaction and you see how much money it pulls out of the marketplace and into your store.

But going back now to our Retail Operating Plan numbers, bounce-back coupons are a markdown. The difference between Back Door Margin and Front Door Margin is markdowns, including bounce-back coupons and everything else. Next, to get to Final Gross Margin, the fourth type of margin, you subtract freight, if you have not already subtracted this, and shrinkage from the Front Door Margin.

While I'm talking again about shrinkage, I'll say that if I looked over your Profit & Loss Statement, I'd want to see a line item for shrinkage reserve on there. I say that because I've learned that there are a lot of retailers who don't take inventories. They don't do perpetual counts. Now I don't know for sure what you're thinking as you read what I just said. I also don't know for sure if you have to report an inventory number at the end of the year to serve as a beginning inventory for the following year. But I do know that I'll often work with retailers who can't get that final inventory number because they don't know what their shrinkage has been in their company. Shrinkage is a real number, and you must include it in your budget.

Back Door Margin minus all of your markdowns equals your Front Door Margin, and Front Door Margin minus shrinkage minus freight equals your Final Gross Margin. Let's say your Back Door Margin is 52% and your margin impact on markdowns is 3 margin points. Your Front Door Margin is then 52% minus 3%, or 49%. If your shrinkage is 3% and your freight and other transportation costs amount to 2%, that makes your Final Gross Margin 44%.

What is the Final Gross Margin in your business? Right now might be a great time to put a piece of paper here in the book as a bookmark and go through the calculations for your situation. But come right back, because we're not yet at the most important number of all.

To get to the Bottom Line Profit, which is the most important number of all in this whole thing, we need to know your Expense Base. This means, for every dollar that goes through your registers, how much of that dollar is used for payroll, occupancy, and all other expenses.

When we talk about payroll, let's be sure we are talking about fully burdened payroll. Fully burdened payroll includes the grand total dollars for the number of hours that your hourly employees work times their respective wages. Then add in the salaries for all of your salaried employees. Now add in the amounts you have to match for any of the employee taxes. Add in the workers' compensation premiums, unemployment insurance premiums, benefits programs. Maybe you have nieces, nephews, brothers, sisters, fathers, daughters who go to school somewhere else, and you cut them a check from the business every week to help them through their school. Include that, too. Fully burdened payroll includes every single penny you spend on the people in your business. For the average Ace Hardware store, payroll is about 21% of sales. The average Home Depot runs at about half of this. That's one reason they make so darn much money.

After payroll, occupancy is the second component of the Expense Base. Occupancy includes rent on the building housing your store. If you own your building, bless you, but you're still paying yourself rent, taxes, insurance, and maintenance on the building. Many people call this "rent plus triple nets." This includes common area maintenance or CAM charges. Some retailers will also add all utility costs into this calculation.

Many retailers I work with give themselves in rent only about 3% of the sales. I don't understand it at all. I'm not a CPA or a tax attorney, but from a tax position, it seems to me that they're far better off to pay themselves fair market rent and get the money that way than they are to take it as a salary and have to pay unemployment taxes on it and things like that. As a guideline, successful retailers need to be below 8% in occupancy. In the hardware industry, it is nearly impossible to make any money at more than 10% occupancy costs unless the owner does not need to draw a salary out of the business. And then, unless you are a multiple store owner, why would you want the store?

I worked with a couple who owned a store in the Midwest. They were struggling badly. The wife looks at the husband and says "All we have here is a hobby. We keep taking money out of our bank account and putting it into the business. When can we start doing the opposite?" Your business may be fun, but it is NOT a hobby!

The third component in the Expense Base is what we call "other expenses." Remember that this does not include principal payback on long-term debt. It does include interest charges. The biggest expense in here for you might be advertising and marketing. The next biggest expense might be bank card charges. That's what you pay for the privilege of using Visa, MasterCard, American Express, and so on. And don't forget travel, interest charges on debt, entertainment, any service contracts you have in the store, and so on. These and the rest of the expenses not already assigned to payroll and occupancy all go into one bucket, and you divide that amount by the amount of sales to give you a percentage. "Other expenses" will cost a retailer about 8% to 12% of their sales.

For my business, the Expense Base totals about 40¢ for every dollar, or 40%. For every dollar that comes into the registers, 40¢ of that dollar goes back to pay expenses. About 20% is payroll, 8% is occupancy, and 12% is all other. I talked before about the value in letting your employees in on how the business works. You can take this giant size replica dollar bill, and you have all your employees sitting around the room, and you ask them, "What percentage of this dollar bill is profit that we can reinvest in the company?" As I mentioned earlier, the average hourly employee would tell you it's 30¢ to 50¢. You go around the room. You have them all guess. Then you say, "Let me tell you how we spend this dollar in this business. The first 55¢ of this dollar bill, that goes to replenish the inventory. We sold it. We've got to buy some more. That's the first 55¢. The next 20¢ goes to payroll."

You can use your own numbers from your business. Then you want you have a chance to explain, because some employees would say, "You don't pay me enough." My reply is usually, "I agree with you. I'd sure like to pay you more. But you know all of those taxes you have to pay? We have to match about 25% of them, and you're covered in case you get in an accident here, that's called workers' compensation, and we've got a little bit of a dental plan and a medical plan for some of the staff and those are benefits that all cost money. It comes to about 20¢ on every dollar. The next 8¢ or so goes to pay the rent and the building expenses. The next 12¢ is all other expenses.

Then after showing my employees how little we have left, I ask them, "How would you like to spend this money that we made last year?" Somebody might say, "I'd sure like to have a pay increase," and then you can go, "There's no money left. The only way in the world we can give pay increases is if we're able to make more money in the business. That's because profits are where pay raises come from."

I tell them that it is just like their checking account. Whether they use a checkbook or use on-line checking, it's no different. If they get a dollar, it goes into the bank account, and they then cut checks back out for utilities, for insurance, for rent, for clothing, for education, for fun. We do the same thing in the business. The numbers are different. The amounts of the checks are different. Where they're going is different, but it's the same concept. And you know what? Most of the employees don't have oodles of money left after the month's over, so the employees get the idea that you might not have oodles of money left over, either.

The Bottom-Line Profit is the Final Gross Margin minus the Expense Base. In this example, that's 45% minus 40%, or a BLP of 5%. Do your own numbers, though. You need to know where you stand. If you told me that there is absolutely no chance in the world that you are upside down, I'd either be laughing or scared. I'd say, "You have got to be kidding me." I know retailers, and I know there are a lot of retailers that were operating upside down, but they just did not know it.

But my real point is that you have to know where you are so you can put that together with where you want to be and then develop and execute your plan to do it. Maybe you would tell me that you wanted your Bottom-Line Profit to be at 6% within one year, but you are not making any money now or are even upside down. Making it to 6% in one year might be tough, so we'd want to set a more realistic objective and build it up to 6% over a longer time. But if you're making 3 points or 4 points and you need another couple of points out there, then we can get them. If you have a goal of 6% and an expense base of 38%, I add those two up, and I immediately know your Final Gross Margin needs to be 44%. If your other figures happen to be the same as ones I used in my example, then I know enough to add your Final Gross Margin to your markdowns, freight, shrinkage at 8%, and I get 52% as the overall Back Door Margin you must have to achieve your objective of 6% Bottom-Line Profit.

Knowledge like that gives you confidence, power, and a competitive advantage, as long as you use the knowledge. So let's use it.

## GOLDEN NUGGETS FOR NOW

- Make a list of every service you do in your business. Make a conscious decision on what services you will charge for and which ones will be free and then SHOUT IT OUT to your customers.
- Clearly state the standards in your business that are nonnegotiable. What is so important to you in your business that if I came and worked for you, unless I did this, I would be fired?
- Train your staff on how a dollar received through your registers is spent by the store.

- If your expense base is higher than your Final Gross Margin, when you do the math, write down the result with a red pen. That's because you're losing money.
- Track your daily, weekly, and monthly Dashboard Indicators.
- Know exactly what you are branding, marketing, and advertising every month. Maintain a very detailed, well thought out plan.
- Use bounce-back coupons.
- Know what your Final Gross Margin is now, what you want or need it to be, and how you will get from where you are now to where you want or need to be.
- Know what your Expense Base (payroll, occupancy, and all other expenses) is now, what you want or need it to be, and how you will get from where you are now to where you want or need to be.

# CHAPTER 7:
# MARGIN MANAGEMENT

*Knowing is not enough; we must apply. Willing is not enough; we must do.*
Johann Goethe (1749–1832)

Margin management is not just something. It is everything. When we think of your business as that vehicle to get you where you want to go, we think of margins as the fuel of your business. Let's tweak your margins a little bit intelligently to put a little bit more money to the bottom line. When I say to do it intelligently, I'll define it specifically for you. I would never, ever price an item to slow down the sales. Never. I want to increase sales just like you do. And I would never price an item to rip off a customer, I would never do that. I would never do anything that would hurt my business, but I want to be smart about my business. I want to understand where I can go into my mix of products to maintain my Back Door Margin at where I need to be to achieve my objectives.

There are three ways to look at every item in your store as it relates to managing your margins. The first way we look at it is called item segmentation. Item segmentation is taking every single item in your database and plugging it into one of four buckets: Sensitive, Competitive, Blind, or Non-comparable.

With items you classify as Sensitive, you need to make a decision: Do you want to be the market leader on price and can you be the market leader on price? If you can't, you must be very close to the market price. Your price should be not more than 5% to 10% above the competition's or market leader's.

With Competitive items, do you want to be the market leader on price and can you be the market leader on price? If you cannot be the market leader, your price should not be more than 10% to 15% above the competition's or market leader's.

How can you tell if an item is to go into the Sensitive or Competitive bucket? Here are the signs:

*Project starter.* In my business, it's gallons of exterior paint or interior paint. I'll drop our margins slightly on our gallons of paint, and then we sell all the sundries, and that's where we're making our money. PVC pipe also goes into my Sensitive or Competitive bucket. PVC pipe, conduit, copper, galvanized. We must be close with the competition on pipe. If we're not, we're going to lose the entire project sale. So we're going to be right where we need to be on pipe, couplings, and elbows. Think what happens if Home Depot is at $1.59 on a 10' stick of PVC pipe, and we take ours to $1.59. Hey, you know what Home Depot will do? They'll be at $1.49. And do you know what happens if we go down to $1.49? Sure you do. They're going down to $1.39. They can afford to take it down to nothing. We're operating small to mid-size retail businesses. We can't afford to take our prices down to nothing, so we have to be careful. If you can lead the market, fine, do it, but if not, just stay within 5% to 15% of the market leader on price.

*Commodity.* These are items you buy and sell by the truckload. For us, it's topsoil, potting soil, bark, steer manure, wood pellets, firewood. We buy truckloads, we sell truckloads. Our margins track down a little bit, and one of the reasons they track down a little bit is those are also items that we are advertising.

*Consumables.* The customers buy it, go home and use it, then buy it again.

*Advertised.* I would not put an item in our ad that Home Depot or Lowe's carried unless we can meet or beat their price. I'll try hard to differentiate in ways other than price whenever possible, but we're not going to put an item out there that is purposely above what they're selling it for.

*Usually bought in multiples.* For us, a good example is cabinet hardware. When a customer is going to buy 10, 20, or 30 of the item at the same time, they are looking closely at price. Now whenever possible, I don't carry the same brand as Home Depot or Lowe's carries, and then I don't need to be so competitive on price. But I still am careful on cabinet latches and the cheap silver polish door pulls.

*Items powered by electricity, batteries, propane, gasoline or rechargeable batteries.* Our margins on these types of items will usually track down.

So that covers the Sensitive and the Competitive buckets. Neither of those yields high margins for us. When it comes to Blind, we have significantly higher margins. Blind items are those SKUs for which few of your customers know the competitors' prices for the items. Non-Comparables are those for which, as far as your customer knows, you are the only one who carries the item, class, or department. Niches, an example of these, provide big opportunities to turn a profit. Why do many hardware stores carry Stihl power equipment in their store? One big reason is that our customers don't find Stihl product in a Home Depot or Lowe's.

With the 28,000 SKUs in my store, we'll be smart in asking for what items do the customers know the competitors' prices and for what items don't they have any idea. Ace Hardware's category management department does a great job in helping with this knowledge. In many cases, the value to the customer of a Blind or Non-Comparable item is set by what the item can do for the customer, not by what the competition might be charging.

Doing the assignment to buckets takes time and experience. For instance, I put most exterior paint gallons into the Sensitive or Competitive bucket, but quarts of exterior paint go into the Blind bucket. To give you an idea of the margin tweaking opportunities in item segmentation, consider the Ace warehouse. My store carries 28,000 SKUs, but there are about 76,000 SKUs that can be ordered from the warehouse. Out of those 76,000, only 500 of them, a fraction of 1%, should be considered as Sensitive, about 11,000, or about 15%, are classified as Competitive, and the other 65,000 SKUs, just under 85%, are Blind or Non-Comparable.

Item segmentation, then, is the first of three approaches to margin management. The second approach is called retail price point or retail price threshold. I'll use my store's experience again as an example, and then you should apply what I'm saying to your store's situation. The average single item sale in my store is under $5.00. This is a very important number to understand in your business because that's where you can focus energies to be able to make a little bit more money in your business.

As the retail price of an item tracks down, say down below $5.00 in my store, it is far more important to be in stock than what the price is, within reason. As the retail price tracks up, pricing becomes more of an issue to the customer. For me, $5.00 is an important price threshold. As the retail price tracks down below $5.00, I am far more concerned about my margins than I am about gross profit dollars. Now, you don't need to be a CPA to realize you cannot take margin to the bank. You take profit dollars if you sell the item. But I sell thousands and thousands of those lower-priced items. Over time, I sell hundreds of thousands of those lower-priced items. About 70% of the items I order for my store sell for retail at less than $10. We start to look at that, and we formulate strategies based on where in our assortment of products we can go to make the money that we need in order to meet our objective for Final Gross Margin.

As the retail price tracks up, let's say over $10.00, I'm more concerned about gross profit dollars than about margin. This is because I don't want to lose the business. I don't want to be out there on a Black & Decker hedge trimmer for $129 when Home Depot is at $99, and the cost to me is $90. I'll be close to Home Depot. I want those gross profit dollars. I'm not going to give away the sale of those types of items, but in our business, it is very important for us to be smart about the margins on lower priced items.

All this leads me to a question for you to answer: In your assortment of products that you carry in your business, looking at price thresholds, price points, or even taking into consideration item segmentation with Blind, Non-Comparable, Sensitive, and Competitive, where are your gross profit dollars coming from that are driving your success? Are they lower priced items, are they higher priced items? Notice that my question is not about where your *sales* come from. I want you to think about where your gross profit dollars come from.

In my business, almost 65% of our gross profit dollars come from Blind and Non-Comparable items that retail for no more than $10.00. Almost 40% of our gross profit dollars are on items below $5.00. So where do we go to look for opportunities to tweak our margins a little bit? We dip down into that lower price because we'll mess around with the prices a little bit more below $5 or below $10. Once we start getting up too high, we're much more sensitive to where the market is.

At the other extreme, less than 3% of our gross profit dollars are from items that are classified as Sensitive. We don't make much money on them. It's not that I don't care about them. Having those items drives traffic into the store, so I want to be right on with pipe, I want to be right on with kerosene. I want that customer shopping in our store, and I'll give away some margin on some of those, but I'm going to make it up somewhere else.

The third approach to margin management is item velocity, which means how quickly or slowly individual products in your store are selling. For this, I bring out another set of buckets, labeled "A" through "D," with "A" being for the fastest selling items, those with the highest inventory turnover, and "D" being for items with the slowest turnover. Oh, yeah, I do have two more buckets for sorting by item velocity. The "X" bucket is for items that have not sold one unit during the past year, just sitting there on your shelf. The "XX" bucket is for the items that have not sold even one unit for at least two years. "XXX" was already taken for use by certain movie producers, so I won't even look inside that bucket for now.

The "X" and "XX" items don't just fail to make you money. They are a downright cost for you, and that gets directly in the way of the profitability we're wanting to build for you. Please most definitely do not say, "Well, I paid $1.00 for it, and I'm not going to sell it unless I get at least $1.00." That does not make any sense. You take it down to half of what you paid for it, you turn it into cash you can reinvest in merchandise that *will* make you money. Once you sell the new item one time, you will nearly make up the difference in lost profit. When you sell it twice, you are already money ahead.

I want to be really clear about this. If you call me up on the phone someday complaining about your cash flow, and you start singing to me that country and western tune, "I Don't Know Where My Money Went," you can expect that I'll sing right back to you my special song called, "Let's Look at Your Obsolete Inventory, Slim." Just like Johnny Cash, I'd be singing about walk the line, but I change the lyrics to make it, "Walk Every Aisle." If I came to consult with you, we'd print a report off if your computer could, and all we'd do is query the system to tell us everything that hasn't sold in the last year. Then we'd go out on the floor and look at it. If you've got inventory numbers in your system, we're going to look at quantities, and we're going to set in place a plan to turn that obsolete inventory into cash so we can reinvest it in the business and make more money.

I know how some retailers think. They say, "I'm not going to sell it below cost. I'm going to sit on it for the next fifty years, and maybe someday somebody might buy it." Well, yes, I agree that somebody might come into your store someday, but by the time they do, chances are you will have lost more money on it than you're going to gain. You will have lost all of your money on that product. There is a cost to carry inventory. Depending on who you talk to, it is anywhere from 1% to 3%. If you have to borrow money to replenish inventory, can you imagine how expensive it is then to keep dead inventory?

I would suggest to you that you tweak margins up on the C and D sellers, but never on the X or XX non-sellers. I'm not talking about putting high margins on items to slow down the sale. Don't hear that. I'm just saying that if you have items on your shelf, and they're selling only a few times per year or less but you must carry them in your store, look at your margins on those items. If you've set a Final Gross Margin overall of 44%, you had better be carrying at least a 50 point margin on those slower selling items. Most definitely, I am not suggesting you or other retailers take arbitrary markups just to improve your gross margin. Be smart about it. Otherwise, do you know what will happen? Some retailers will just go nuts with it, and it can put you out of business. Remember, setting and achieving a gross margin is one of the top priorities a store owner has. There are two key words here in this success formula: "setting" and "achieving." Without both, you will lose.

Let me come at this from a different angle: Remember how I said that success depends on you distinguishing yourself by being the biggest, the least expensive, the most distinctive in merchandise assortment, the best at customer service, or best of all, a mix of those? Well, being a small to midsize business, you have to include the "best at customer service," and only retailers in that category who execute legendary customer service deserve to maximize their profitability. You must earn the right to maximize your profitability, and the way you earn your right is by servicing the customer beyond anybody else in the industry. I've already told you about what happen to be three of the top five tactics for retail pricing. Those three are using item segmentation, item price thresholds, and item velocity. But the one that happens to be right at the top of the top five is outstanding customer service. And please let me repeat myself here: In a service industry, only retailers who execute legendary customer service day in and day out deserve the benefits of maximizing their profitability. You have to earn the right to charge higher prices than the market leader.

Wait, there's that fifth one I haven't told you about yet. It is using a rounding tactic. In fact, if the item segmentation, item price thresholds, and item velocity sound a little overwhelming to start, you should begin with a rounding tactic. Once that's in place, you can tackle the others. And whenever you do use the other three, finish it off with a rounding tactic.

So what's a rounding tactic? Well, let me answer your question with a question: If a customer sees an item priced at $4.99, which number in that price does a customer use to make their buying decision?

The correct answer: The $4. A customer will make a buying decision on the number to the *left* of the decimal. They own that number. As the retailers, you and I own the numbers to the right of the decimal, whether its $.29, $.49, $.79, $.95, $.99, or whatever. So since we own those numbers, whenever possible let's always make them $.99 instead of $.95. We're not talking chump change here. We're not talking a thousand dollars, we're not talking two thousand dollars, we're talking about thousands and thousands and thousands of dollars, and we're talking about it because we're very fortunate. We have thousands of items, we run thousands of transactions. Do the math. When I've done the math with store owners, the store owner will discover an aggressive rounding scheme can be worth 2 to 4 margin points for nothing more than price rounding. Be sure to round everything in your store. Not just your core departments, but also your niches. Use a well thought out rounding tactic on *every* item in your store.

The retailer owns the number to the right of the decimal. It contributes to the profit in my business. But since the customer owns the number to the left of the decimal, the $4 in my example, I'm going to be very cautious in how I change that number. This ties in with my attention to pricing thresholds. Remember that I want to maximize the profitability, but do it without slowing down the sale.

| If the current price is: | Set the price at: |
|---|---|
| Between $1.00 and $2.00 | $1.29, $1.49, $1.79 or $1.99 |
| Between $2.01 and $3.00 | $2.49 or $2.99 |
| Between $3.01 and $5.00 | $3.49, $3.99, $4.49 or $4.99 |
| Between $5.01 and $10.00 | $5.99, $6.99, $7.99, $8.99 or $9.99 |
| Between $10.01 and $15.00 | $11.99, $12.99 or $14.99 |
| Between $15.01 and $20.00 | $16.99, $18.99 or $19.99 |
| Between $20.01 and $35.00 | $21.99, $24.99, $29.99 or $34.99 |
| Between $35.01 and $55.00 | $39.99, $44.99, $49.99 or $54.99 |
| Between $55.01 and $75.00 | $59.99, $64.99, $69.99 or $74.99 |
| Between $75.01 and $100.00 | $79.99, $89.99 or $99.99 |

Here's the rounding tactic that works for me. On items below $1, we use a lot of different price points. But once we get above $1, from $1.00 to $2.00, we'll use $1.29, $1.49, $1.79, or $1.99. We do not use $1.29 or $1.79 very often. You know why? We've learned over the years that it does not matter. Okay, I know there are exceptions to this, but we handle the exceptions and move on. What is mostly true is that there is not a customer around who would pay $1.79 for the product, but would not pay $1.99. I'd rather have that $.20 in my cash register than in the customer's pocket, so I'll charge $1.99.

I am not telling you to be ridiculous about this. If you need to be at $1.49 on a Sensitive or Competitive item, that's where you should be. But if you tell me you could sell as many at $1.99, then all I'd do is look you right directly in the eye and go, "Then, why aren't you at $1.99? Couldn't you use the money?" Hey, I'll back right off if you say that you have half a million dollars sitting in your yard right now, investments overseas, and a Brink's truck coming past your store five times a day to pick up all the money you're making. But otherwise, I'm going to be asking you why in heck you want to leave all those thousands and thousands and thousands of pennies and dimes in the customers' pockets instead of in your cash registers. Watch the pennies closely, and the dollars will follow.

When you start working on retail pricing in your store, begin by looking at your sales by department and then by product class. Focus on the departments and then classes where most of your sales are coming from. The lesson here is for you to keep very close track of every single class in the store. Within each product class, set up pricing tactics or pricing strategies for your items that are Sensitive, Competitive, Blind, and Non-Comparable. Set up the tactics or strategies for lower-priced items, let's say items that have a cost below $10.00. And if nothing else, use a rounding tactic.

Look again at how it works. Between $2 and $3, we have just $2.49 and $2.99. That's it. No $2.79? Nope. No $2.60? That's right. Why? Well, by now, you know why.

Couldn't you use the added money? Don't you need the money? It takes a tremendous amount of money to be a great retailer. It is not cheap. If you want to grow the business, and, hey, you need to grow your business, it takes that much more money. And you know what? The customers want you to be successful. They want your store to be there, convenient to them. They want to be able to shop with you. They want you to grow.

Going back to the rounding tactic, you won't find many items at all in our store at $4.49. That's because $5 is a critical pricing threshold for the customer's mind, so we'll take the price right up to that level, but not to $5. When I jump from $4.99, I'm going to $5.99. What's the difference in price to a customer on an item marked $5.19 instead of $4.99? It is one dollar. You say, "Wait, it's only 20¢, not $1.00." No, it is $1. Customers use the number to the left of the decimal to make their buying decisions.

In a million years, I would not price an item at $5.09, $5.10, or $5.15 unless I was Wal-Mart, where I'm making my strongest case on price. But my store is distinctive on customer service and merchandise assortment. If I saw a bin tag in *my* store that read $5.09, $5.10, or $5.15, I would faint. Right there in the aisle, I would faint dead away. My wife, Geni, who operates the store, would have to call Jim, the assistant manager, who we call Big Jim, to carry me out through the back door and toss me in the Dumpster so the customers aren't tripping over me. Geni is really good about avoiding safety hazards in our store.

Yes, $5.00 is a critical threshold. We'll play with the prices between $2 and $5, we'll play with them a little bit, but when we jump $5, I'll tell you, we're very, very careful. When we jump $10, we're going to $11.99. What about $10.99? Two reasons you don't go to $10.99. First off, it's a tax form number in the United States , and nobody likes the U.S. Internal Revenue Service. Second, I would tell you there is not a customer in the world who will give you $10.99 and won't give you $11.99. Now they might not give you $11.99 because in their mind it was a $9.99 item, but if they'll pay $10.99, they'll pay $11.99.

Okay, there are exceptions. There are a few customers who would pay $10.99, but not $11.99. But remember, I don't operate my business on exceptions. I operate on what is true most of the time. Also, $10.99 could work if Scott's Summerizer was at Home Depot for $10.99. There's a good chance that I'd meet them on that price, but again, it would be the exception, not the rule. And I make an exception for sequencing. If I have the 6 oz. size at $1.99 and the 12 oz. size at $2.99, and I see there's a demand for a 9 oz. size, I might bring it into the store and price it at $2.79 so the pricing makes sense to the customer.

When we jump $15, we're going to $16.99. I don't stop at $13.99 because lots of people consider 13 to be an unlucky number, and customers own the number to the left of the decimal. I don't stop at $15.99 because I challenge you to show me the customer who will give me $15.99, but not $16.99. They're just not out there.

We don't use $109.99. We go $119.99, $129.99, $149.99, $179.99, $199.99. Once we get over $200, we're going $229.99, $249.99, $279.99, $299.99. From $300 to $700, we are only at $349.99 and $399.99, and so on. Once we get over $700, we're rolling a hundred dollars at a time.

Before you disagree, think for a second here. Think this through carefully. A well thought out and executed rounding scheme is worth thousands and thousands of profit dollars to a retailer. This is serious money and can be the difference between success and failure. Our financial model will not allow us to be competitive on every item we sell. Outstanding service comes with a price.

What if customers ask you why your prices are higher than at the competition? Well, first of all, realize the customers expect prices at the high-convenience, world-class-service, small to midsize retail business to be higher than at the Big Boxes. Even when we're priced below the Big Boxes, we get no credit for this. They will think our prices are significantly higher than at a Big Box. So I say, why disappoint them?

But answering questions about pricing is another place where scripting for the floor staff and cashiers is helpful. Here's what I suggest as an answer. "Thank you for your input. I'll let my manager know what you've said. I think you'll find that our prices are fair, and we are where we need to be to offer the services for our community."

The problem you have here is when you do not execute on what the customers' expectations are. They will pay a higher price if there is value attached to it. If your customers are complaining about your higher prices, maybe what they are saying is, "I would pay a higher price in your store, but I do not see a benefit to do this, so I may as well shop at a Big Box."

I think you see that margin management and the other parts of setting retail prices require a constant focused effort. I wouldn't want to make margin management sound easier than it is. Margin management is a journey, not a destination. In my store, I have an employee who serves as our Retail Pricing Specialist. His job responsibilities are completely devoted to managing the retail price changes in the store. His name is Bob, and unlike what I've done with almost all the other names in this book, I'm so proud of Bob that I'm using his real name. As I've said a few times already, I'd never tell you that what I do in my business or what somebody else does in their business is always the very best way for you to do business. In describing Bob and what Bob does, I want to share an idea that might work very well for you, or you might adapt it in some way to work even better for you than it has for me.

Bob puts up the bin tags with the new prices on them. Bob is authorized to recruit help if he's got a very large price change, but by and large, it is Bob who puts up the bin tags, and it is always Bob who takes responsibility for the bin tags being perfect. Bob knows about product locations in the store. And to pull it all together, Bob overflows with high-quality common sense.

Once each year, Bob does category reviews and pricing reviews on all of our critical classes of merchandise. He shops the local competition as necessary, and he makes sure the retail price changes will make sense to the customer. That is truly important. For instance, think about what we call "runs and relationships." Think about drill bits. The customer expects the price to go up as the size of the drill bit goes up. They'll think it's a mistake if the prices go up and down as they look at the same brand of drill bit with increasing sizes. That could give us a poor pricing image. So when Bob puts up the bin tags, he just sort of steps back and looks them over. Does it always go 1, 2, 3 for the same price, go up, do 1, 2, 3, go up, 1, 2, 3, go up?

A really big benefit in having somebody do retail pricing in our stores comes when there's a pile of bin tags out on the sales floor. Employees who prefer to be doing lots of other things than put up bin tags end up putting up those tags as fast as they can so they can get that sheet clear and just throw it away. In doing it that way, they are missing one very important element: Once those bin tags are up, they forget to stand back, look, and spot the places where you have to say, "That would not make sense to the customer." You'd be impressed by how many thousands and thousands and thousands of dollars we've made in our company just by having Bob stand back to look at the relationships among the item prices.

Sometimes Bob will monitor sales on our "A" items, our best-sellers. If we take a price increase, I get nervous, and I ask Bob to monitor those for a few months. I never ask him to manage more than 100 price changes at a time, and I have him monitor those just to make sure that if we take a price increase, our sales don't go down. I don't want to let that happen.

Bob has great initiative. He looks for and finds margin opportunities. He understands the need for profit and is motivated to have our store succeed. He's detail-oriented, excellent at follow through, computer literate, and able and willing to learn. Those are strengths for you to look for if you decide to hire a Retail Pricing Specialist.

Every hour they work, they're making money. Bob is not a cost to our business. He's an investment. Yes, we do pay him, but I would argue that, by definition, it is an investment to your business, even though you put out money, when you make much more money than you put out. Their efforts are multiplied every single day, day after day, year after year. Bob's been doing retail pricing for us since 1995, the year after I caught the margin management fever. Oh, yes, one more thing: Do not even think about coming into my store and trying to steal Bob. Find or develop your own Bob.

Bob is so important to our store that if the business ever got really, really bad, and there were only two people left in our store, it would be Bob and me. I also set a special set of standards for Bob. You know by now how important standards are to me. I expect employees to show up on time and put in the hours they agreed to work. But I don't tell Bob, "You'll work Monday, Tuesday, Wednesday." I don't say to Bob, "You're going to work 24 hours this week." There are price changes Bob gets on Monday that have to be done on Friday. I don't care when he does them. It doesn't matter to me when he does them as long as they get done. I can accept that arrangement because I know Bob carries lots of initiative and he's well organized.

In addition to a Retail Pricing Specialist, I suggest you have software to help with the margin management process. An excellent example of this category of software, and the one that I use in *our* business, is Margin Master by RetailerSoft. Here are the sorts of features I recommend you look for in technology for margin management, based on what I've said so far and what you'll read me saying in later chapters:

The ability to easily input basic product information, such as department, class, product group, item code, item description, vendor data, cost, retail price, and monthly sales amounts.

The ability to easily drill down from the product class level towards the item level in order to determine where in your assortment of products you can go to achieve the best Bottom-Line Profit.

Allows easy identification of items that carry a margin or a sales velocity that is lower than what you consider to be acceptable.

Sets rules for rounding off prices in ways that maximize your profitability on every item sold without losing sales.

Allows numerous "what-if" scenarios without committing to actually making the changes.

Quickly calculates the annual and month-by-month dollar and sales percentage impacts of "what-if" changes in pricing.

Quickly calculates results by store, department, supplier, or other ways you categorize your inventory.

Saves retail pricing strategies so that you can call them up later without needing to recreate the strategy each time your product mix changes.

Smoothly interfaces with a way to produce bin tags containing the new prices.

Allows you to see at a glance where the gross profit dollars in your company are coming from as it relates to item segmentation, item price thresholds, and item velocity.

Is backed by a company that has support staff who are available, willing, friendly and knowledgeable with experience in your type of business.

Your retail pricing software needs to save you time, give you 100% accuracy, and make you more money. When I use Margin Master, it has my sales history from last year, so it predicts the future based on my last year's history. I hit the Apply button, and within seconds, it tells me how much more money I'm going to put to the bottom line if I make this change, whatever the change is. This is a powerful tool to help manage the retail pricing process.

In 1994, I was close to going out of business, really close to going out of business. I was struggling big time. Then I started to get this whole margin management thing, and man, one day I woke up, and that old light just clicked on, and I haven't stopped smiling since because once you get it, you know margin management is a process. I selected Bob to manage the retail pricing because I quickly discovered you don't ever finish creating the profit-making potentials from margin management. Once you start on it and get involved with it, it's not something you start today and finish. You never, ever, ever stop working on it. Sometimes it is a slow, tedious process. But at the end of the day, it's excellent for your profitability, and that's more than enough to keep me going with it. The more time I spend working on retail pricing, the more money I make.

I don't fully understand why there are retailers who do not want to take the margin management steps to make more money. There are retailers who won't do anything more than double the supplier's cost of the item to set the price at retail. Are you among them? If so, I would tell you cost is only a guide, that's all. What is most important to you is what the market will bear, which means recognizing what value the customer sees in the item, the service that goes along with the item, the convenience you offer to the customer, and all the rest. What you pay the supplier for the item goes into it, and we look at that with the Back Door Margin. But do not be afraid to mark something up to more than double the cost if that is what customers will pay because that's the value they set on having the item.

Take your thinking back to being a professional instead of an amateur. I have retailers telling me it is not their job to set prices, it's the supplier's job. I have retailers who say they don't want to take on margin management because they don't have the time or the right people to do it for them. I say, do not allow somebody else to impact your success to that degree. I say to those retailers, "Whose job is it to prevent you from going out of business?" I know the government might subsidize the airlines, bail out the banks, and keep the auto industry alive. But do you think that if you or I have big financial problems in our businesses, the government is going to rescue us? No way. At least, I'm sure not counting on it. They're going to want the dime I wasn't able to pay them last year, and they're going to want twice as much in interest on it this year. So take personal accountability. Monitor your Dashboard Indicators. Use the information your systems give you that empower you to make the best decisions for your business.

## GOLDEN NUGGETS FOR NOW

- Formulate strategies based on where in your assortment of products you can go to make the money that you need in order to meet your objective for Final Gross Margin.
- Be sure that you consistently go beyond setting a gross margin to truly achieving that gross margin.
- Earn the right to charge higher prices than the market leader. In a service industry, only retailers who execute legendary customer service day in and day out deserve the benefits of maximizing their profitability.
- Use a well thought out rounding tactic on EVERY item in your store, not just your core departments, but also your niches.

- Do not be afraid to mark down an item to below cost if that is what it will take to clear it out.
- Watch the pennies closely, and the dollars will follow.
- Have a Retail Pricing Specialist in your store.
- Get and then use retail pricing software that will save you time and make you more money.

# CHAPTER 8:
# BEYOND MARGIN
# MANAGEMENT

*The worst crime against working people is a company
which fails to operate at a profit.*
Samuel Gompers (1908)

Keep thinking about the Retail Pyramid of Profit. We've been talking about the Retail Operating Plan, which is at the base, but there is lots more in the RPOP. There are eight other essential elements, and each of them ties together with the Retail Operating Plan to build your profitability. Consider Product Selection and Top-of-Mind Awareness, for instance.

If you want to have some fun one day, take a camera and walk through your store. Just start shooting photographs of your store. Shoot a lot of them. Load all of them up on your computer, and sit in front of your computer with your staff, and ask, "What do you see? Where are our opportunities? What does our store look like?" Sit there and find ways to make your store better.

If you intend to sell a lot of paint, what does your paint department look like? As you look at the photos, and as you walk by the paint department itself, how are you making it inviting for the customers to come there and buy? Do you want your end caps to be signed? Do you want the end caps to be full? What do you want the end caps to look like? What do you want the main aisle to look like? What do you want the impulse areas at the registers to look like? What do you want your store front to look like? Take those pictures and look carefully at them with your managers and your floor staff, because what you see is what you are going to get. If you want it to be different, then have it look different. What do you want all your aisles to look like? Is the store merchandised in a way that shows off the product categories in which you want to be dominant?

In my business, spray paint is a place where we want to be dominant. Garden hoses are a huge category for my store. In the greater Sacramento market area, we are very strong in the garden hose department. Home Depot's garden hose department might look decent, but I can tell you that their garden hose department won't be nearly as complete as ours is. What do you aim to have as your dominant categories? If I looked at the photos you took in your store, would I be able to tell?

What's the competition doing? If you're competing against Bunning's in Australia, don't go up against them on wheelbarrows. I have never seen a company that did wheelbarrows better than Bunning's does. If you want a wheelbarrow, you're probably going down to Bunning's because they have one heck of a great selection there. And their display techniques are excellent.

Try this out: Stand in front of your store and ask yourself, "Why should a customer shop in my store?" Do the same thing in every department. There must be specific reasons why a customer would drive past a Big Box and shop with you. And what do you do in your business that will take a customer out of your competition and put them in your store? The answer to this question can make you a lot of money.

Sometimes you start selling a product and get surprised by its popularity, so you decide to feature it as you lay out the merchandise. That happened to us with a product called Gorilla Glue. It is unbelievably strong and unbelievably popular. The way I take care of certain employees in our business is to sneak it onto their napkins at one of our store pizza parties. When they wipe their face, you never have to listen to them again. That stuff is strong.

The number one selling item at our cash registers is balsa wood airplanes. Did you put those together and fly them when you were a kid? Great fun, right? Where do you go to buy them now for your own kids and grandkids? You can't find them? We couldn't find them either, but we kept searching. When we hit pay dirt, we started stocking them in the store. These days, we sell hundreds and hundreds a year. You know, you wind them all up and then you let them go, and either the rubber band breaks or the blade breaks, so they've got to buy another one. So maybe it's only two or three customers buying the hundreds a year, but, hey, it brings those guys into the store.

The number two selling item at our registers is a skin cream called Anti Monkey Butt, but most people ask for it as Monkey Butt. You don't want to know where it comes from. I mean, you don't want to know what they make it from. But to find out where it comes from so we could carry it, I had to go to the internet. Our number three register area seller is Grandma's Lye Soap. And right up there in the top group is Teflon tape. If you sell threaded stuff in your stores, like hose bibs and galvanized fittings, set up a small display of Teflon tape at the register. Then train your cashiers so that every single time a customer comes up to the register with anything that is threaded, okay, not nuts and bolts, the cashier reaches down into the bowl, picks up a roll, and says to the customer, " Do you need any Teflon tape to stop that from leaking? It's only $1.29." Since we began having our cashiers do that, half the customers buying threaded items add on the Teflon tape. Now, as you're reading me telling you this, I'll bet you are saying, "Art, everybody in the world has at least six rolls of Teflon tape in their garage already." Okay, you are right, but I'm shooting for ten.

The customers coming into your store might not be looking for house paint, spray paint, garden hoses, Anti Monkey Butt, Grandma's Lye Soap, or Teflon tape. But you get the idea of what I mean. Think about what products make money for you, and then stock them. Think about how powerful it would be to know all of the products that you carry that are not carried by your competition. This lets you differentiate in the market. You know where to go to find out what you can carry to meet the customer demands, right? Yes, ask the customers and ask your employees. When is the last time you checked with your employees to discover what the customers ask for that you do not carry? They will tell you if you ask.

Be creative in building that Top-of-Mind Awareness. Do you go over to your competition, not just to walk through the stores regularly, but also to drive through the parking lot? Write down the names and phone numbers of the businesses that are in your competition's parking lots. Then come back to your store and have your outside sales person, you yourself, or somebody else contact those people to say, "Hey, you know what? You've got to come down here to our store. We have an excellent trade program. We're a smaller store. We carry only 28,000 items in the store, but we can get you 100,000 items. Would you be offended if I send you some information in the mail?"

Do you know what people say when you ask, "Would you be offended if I send you information in the mail?" They say no, I would not be offended. So you say, "Okay, cool, I'll call you back in a week, after you get it." And go beyond doing it in the parking lots of your competitors. Do it in your own parking lot, too, because a lot of those people who are shopping are business-to-business shoppers, but you don't know that because they don't yet have an account with you. They have an account or accounts somewhere else. They're coming into your store to pick up one or two items, and then they're leaving. Get their business names from their trucks or cars in your parking lot. Look up the phone numbers, get in contact with them, and build those relationships.

Keep Top-of-Mind Awareness for you and for your staff, too. To let you know what I mean by that, I'll back up a bit. I've told you about the value of scripts, such as what the salesperson says and does in greeting and in thanking every customer and in answering questions about pricing. I've told you about nonnegotiable standards. One very important standard, and it has to do with actions the employee takes, is "It takes two to say no, but only one to say yes." That's a motto to put on a poster in BIG LETTERS in the employee break room and to show on the BIG SCREEN at every staff meeting and training session for employees.

Why is that motto so important? Well, have you ever said no to a customer only to find out a minute, an hour, a day later that the correct answer was yes, but you just didn't know it? If you have ever worked on the sales floor, I'm pretty sure it has happened to you. You can bet that it happened to me dozens of times. It happens to us because we don't know what we don't know. You and I are not telling the customer no because we don't want to help the customer. Maybe some of your employees do it for that reason, but I don't think we do. We say no because we truly believe that we don't have the product or we're not able to provide the service the customer is asking for.

But whatever the reason for the no, let's change things in ways that make the customer happier and make us some money. A customer comes into the store, they ask an employee a question, the employee wants so bad to say no to the customer, but they are not allowed to. We slow down the process. We slow it down to a crawl. That employee must check with another employee before they say no.

Hey, I told you at the start of this book that it's okay if you call me an idiot. Is now the time? I can sort of imagine you saying, "I've got people in the store who have been with me for twenty years, and they know everything in the store." Yes, but it is not the *employee* I'm concerned about. It's the *customer*. I want the customer to be respected in the business. How do you do that? You go to every length you can to take care of them. I have seen employees say no so fast that the customer's hair turns from black to grey and as soon as they pass by a mirror, they sprint right out of the store, never to return. Think about it. When you walk into a store, and you ask an employee something, and they say no really fast, what goes through your mind? I'll tell you what's going through my mind. "How can you be so sure? Do they really care?"

For example, a customer comes in, walks up to Alex, who was hired last week, and asks nicely, "Do you carry a left-handed stickledickle?" From the blank look on Alex's face, the customer is thinking, "I'm pretty sure they carry one of those, but this sales guy doesn't recognize what it is because he's so much younger than I am."

As far as Alex knows, no left-handed stickledickle is anywhere in the store. Alex is even thinking that this customer is playing around with Alex's mind, using a crazy name like stickledickle. Alex is all ready to say NO! in a loud voice. But I want Alex to say instead, "I'm going to check on that so I can be sure to give the right answer." Alex uses his radio to call a more experienced employee, Fred, to ask him the customer's question. The customer sees and hears Alex doing this and can't help but be impressed that Alex is going the extra mile instead of just saying no.

But I'll be honest with you that it's lucky the customer can't hear Fred on the other end of the radio conversation because Fred is laughing so hard. When Fred finally calms down, he says, "No, I'm sure we don't have that in stock, and I think that's really a silly name for a product. In this store, we carry only products with more dignified names, like Monkey Butt, but I suggest you take the customer to our service desk and see if a left-handed stickledickle is listed in our special order catalog."

We've slowed down the no process to a crawl. We might slow it even more, and make an important sale, if Alex says, "I can't find that listed in the catalog, but please tell me what you plan to use it for and if you think it might go by some other names so I can find one of our products that is sure to do the job for you." Then Alex might need to get on the radio again to ask Fred if the store has the right product in stock or can get it.

I told you about Big Jim. He's the one who's going to drag me out to the Dumpster when I faint in the aisle. Jim and I have worked together since 1976, way before I started American River Ace Hardware. When I opened up my business, Jim was one of the first people I hired. Jim is the assistant manager in our store. Even with all that, Jim won't say no to a customer without checking with somebody else. Big Jim knows as much about that store as anybody else does, but what he's going to do is say, "I don't think so, but I'm going to double-check for you." Respect is what it shows.

There was a period of time in our business when I did all the ordering for the store. Remember the Amateur? I was the owner of the store, but sometimes I was an Amateur. The first years in the business, I was right there. I knew more about the stock in the store than anybody else did. But I didn't know everything there was to know about the business. I didn't know how all the items we carried could be used. I didn't understand that. So a customer comes in and asks, "Do you carry two-gallon trash bags?" I say that we don't. After the customer leaves, I'm thinking we might want to start carrying two-gallon trash bags. I ask one of my employees about it, and he says, "Art, what in the heck is wrong with you? Rucksack bags are right there on Aisle 7." Oh, Rucksack bags are two-gallon trash bags.

And that brings it to the point I want to make about Top-of-Mind Awareness for the store staff and owner/operator. But first, I've something to tell you in case you haven't already figured it out for yourself. There's a tool I carry in my store that looks like a screwdriver, but it's threaded at the end. It is used by craftsmen to start the screw holes when they're putting together handcrafted wood cabinets. One reason I carry the product is that I want my merchandise selection to be distinctive. You aren't likely to find that tool on the shelves at Lowe's Home Center or at The Home Depot, for instance. If you don't believe me, go into one of those stores and ask for it by name. Old-time carpenters call it a stickledickle.

Well, okay, I made up the "left-handed" part.

Tying all I've been talking about into Top-of-Mind Awareness for the store staff and for you has to do with something that Bruce Sanders and I call the "Yes, I Can" form. Maybe in your store you call it a Lost Sales Form. Whenever one of your store staff does, in fact, need to say no to a customer after checking with at least one other person, how do you know it? How do you get the valuable feedback like that so you can improve your business and increase your profitability? Ask the employee to write it down and then give the form to the store manager. That's all we require them to do. We don't challenge the employee on it. Once we chew somebody out because they filled out one of those forms, they'll never fill out another one in their life. If they pick up one of those forms because they said no, but the correct answer is yes, that points out a training and coaching need. It's valuable information.

Here's something I'll guarantee: If you take this seriously, you will use the information from about 25% of these that get turned in. You'll find out your people are saying no for things where the correct answer is yes. You'll also find out that your customers are asking for products that you're not aware that they're asking for. You'll find out that there are services you could be offering in your market that the customers want you to do, and you just don't know about it. And what I've seen happen often is that the employees are not aware of all the services offered by the store. They've forgotten, or maybe they've never been told, about the soil testing, saw blade sharpening, window shade cutting, or whatever other services you can offer that distinguish you from the competition. The "Yes, I Can" form gives you, your managers, and your floor staff really valuable Top-of-Mind Awareness.

So now we've brought Services into it. That's one more of the elements in the Retail Pyramid of Profit. When was the last time you sat down with the smartest people in your store and made a list of every single service that you do for the customers? In a store like mine, this includes paint mixing and key cutting. Whatever kind of store you operate, you might assemble products, handle special orders, and wrap gifts.

Next question: When was the last time you carefully decided how much to charge the customer for services and what they get for free? I'll argue all day that you absolutely do not need to give away everything. Put a reasonable price on it. I've come across stores that still charge only $3.50 to rekey a Kwikset lock. In my market area, the going rate is about $10, and the customer considers that a fair value. If you get it done at Home Depot in my market area, and they will do it, it takes about three to four days. At American River Ace, we do it in one day. Yes, if they buy the locks from us, we'll do it for free.

After you get that list of services and decide what, if anything, you will charge for each, list them on one side of one piece of standard size paper, like in three columns. At the top, put the title "Community Services" and add the phone number of your store, but not the name of your store. Make a few copies of that sheet and laminate each copy. Next, visit each of your Big Box competitors who has a community bulletin board. You know where I'm going with this. Take whatever is on that bulletin board in the top right-hand corner and very neatly put it somewhere else on the bulletin board so you can put up your list in its place. Next, walk away with a smile on your face. That smile is there because you'll be taking customers out of the competition's business and putting them into your business.

A customer sees an item on that list of services and calls us on the phone. I say, "Good morning, American River Hardware. This is Art. How may I direct your call?" On the other end of the line, I hear, "Do you guys do re-screening of window screens?" "Yes we do." "Gee, I'm down here at Home Depot, and I got your phone number from them. I've got a screen here. How long is it going to take to get it done?" "It's 4 PM, so if you bring it in right now, we'll have it done by tomorrow morning." "Okay, I'm driving to your store right now." A customer out of Home Depot and into American River Ace.

If you have a moral objection to doing things this way, you could put the idea into the "golden nuggets not used" bucket. But before you do that, I ask that you consider the endless number of ways that the Big Boxes are doing the same kinds of things to you. Maybe you don't always know what they are doing to you, but still, they are doing them. You have your creditors out there, and they want you to pay your bills. You need the money, the Big Boxes have plenty of chances to make their money, and those guys with the window screens to be repaired appreciate finding somebody to get the job done so quickly. Services can be a great differentiator. Shout it out to your customers.

There's a hardware retailer in Georgia. The Home Depot comes in right across the street from them, directly across the street, no exaggeration. I'm meeting with this retailer because they went from $2.0 million to $1.1 million in sales in one year. The retailer's business lost over $250,000 for the year. So now I'm at the store with him trying to figure out what in the world happened here. Around the corner and down the street from this hardware store is a small competitor, not more than a half mile away. What I found out was that the competitor's store flat out owned the services in this market area. They owned them. They owned screening, they owned glass cutting, they owned every single service, and the competitor's store owner knew a year ahead of time that Home Depot was coming in, so they just kept building and building that services business. The hardware retailer I was meeting with took about a 45% hit. The competitor retailer took about a 10% hit. All the nine elements of the RPOP work together, and in addition to Services, what that competitor retailer did was a matter of Leadership.

# GOLDEN NUGGETS FOR NOW

- Start shooting lots of photographs of your store. Load all of them up on your computer. Then sit in front of your computer with your staff, and ask, "What do you see? Where are our opportunities? What does our store look like?"
- Stand in front of your store and ask yourself, "Why should a customer shop in my store?" Do the same thing in every department. Always know exactly what you do in your business that will take a customer out of your competition and put them in your store.
- If you sell threaded items in your stores, set up a small display of Teflon tape at each register. Then train your cashiers so that every time a customer comes up to the register with anything that is threaded, okay, not nuts and bolts, the cashier reaches down into the bowl, picks up a roll, and says to the customer, "Do you need any Teflon tape to stop that from leaking? It's only $1.29."
- Regularly ask your employees, "What are the customers asking for that we don't carry?" Have staff complete a "Yes, I Can" form or a Lost Sales Form whenever one of your store staff does, in fact, need to say no to a customer after checking with at least one other person.
- Go over to your competition, not just to walk through the stores regularly, but also to drive through the parking lot. Write down the names and phone numbers of the businesses that are in your competition's parking lots. Then come back to your store and have your outside sales person, you yourself, or somebody else contact those people to say, "Hey, you know what? You've got to come down here to our store. We have an excellent trade program. We're a

smaller store. We carry only 28,000 items in the store, but we can get you 100,000 items. Would you be offended if I send you some information in the mail?"

- Be sure that every employee in your store knows all that we mean by, "It takes two to say no, but only one to say yes."
- On community bulletin boards at Big Box stores, post a list of services your store offers. At the top, have the title "Community Services" and include the phone number of your store, but not the name of your store.
- To discover good ways to improve your business, ask your employees these questions:

  1. What makes our store a great place to work?
  2. What would make our store a better place to work?
  3. What makes our store a great place for customers to shop?
  4. What would make our store a better place to shop?
  5. What are customers asking for that we do not currently stock?

# CHAPTER 9:
# CREATING ADVOCATES

*Your most unhappy customers are your greatest source of learning.*
Bill Gates (1955 - )

If you want to improve the perception your customers have of your pricing, improve your customer service.

I know I'm really simplifying about this, but from the way I think about it, there are only three types of customers you can create—an Advocate, an Adversary, and a Ho-Hum. The Advocates just love your store, they love your staff, and if they've had a chance to meet you, the owner/operator, they love you, too. They have tremendous loyalty, and that comes because they've been treated well. Advocates stay in your store longer than Adversaries or Ho-Hums, and they buy more whenever they are in your store. Then when they leave your store, they tell other people what a great job you did. This is the best form of advertising you can have, word of mouth.

The Adversary is at the other extreme. They hate you. When they leave your store, they tell other people what a terrible job you did. Now maybe that's because your store did do a terrible job. But whatever, once the Adversaries have it in their heads that your store is no good, they keep believing that. They don't come into the store again to give you a chance to change their minds, or if they do come in, it's just to pick out the negatives so they have more to criticize you about. One of the bad problems with Adversaries is that only about one out of ten will tell you or the people in the store what they think of you. The other 90% or so go around chasing people away from your store without giving you the chance to change their minds. Adversaries are the worst advertising you can have.

The third category, the Ho-Hums, are the customers who come into your store, shop, consider it an average experience, don't see anything great about the store, don't see anything poor about the store, and go on their way. What makes Ho-Hums interesting to me is that these are the customers we have a chance to turn into Advocates. What's also interesting is that our best opportunities to turn them into Advocates is when they have a problem with the store. If a customer has a problem in your store, and they take it up a level to management, and then that manager takes care of them, they become more loyal than they were before they had the problem.

I'll give you an example of how it worked for me. I travel all the time, so I rent cars. I've dealt with every car rental company on earth almost. But now whenever I need to rent a car, I rent from National. You see, before I'd made the decision to give all my business to National, I'd rented a car from them in Chicago. The next morning, I got up, went out to the car, and found that the battery was dead, completely dead. I was mad at National for giving me this car. I was all ready to become an Adversary of National Car Rental. I get a cab and go to the office, where I call National to tell them what had happened. The woman who answers the phone asks me what time I'll be back at the car. I tell her it will be at 6:00 PM. She says, "As soon as you get there, call me so I can send somebody out." I tell her that won't work at all because I have an airplane to catch at 7:30 PM, so I need to be driving the car at 6:00 PM.

Her response was, "Well, we can't do that for you." You can't do that for me? That started me thinking about the things I could not do for National Car Rental, such as renting cars from them. I said, "Let me talk to your manager, please." I wasn't rude. And what I heard next were the most wonderful words in the world. The woman said into my ears by way of the telephone, "Mr. Freedman, what can we do to make this right?"

I asked her to have somebody at the place the car was at when I arrived at 6:00 PM so I could get into the car immediately and drive to the airport. She said, "It's done. All you'll need to do is sign the document for the replacement car." My whole attitude towards National had changed in seconds. I thanked her. In fact, I remember saying, "That is wonderful." I made it through the day, took a cab back so I was there by 6:00 PM, signed the paperwork, got into the new car they'd brought for me, and I was on my way to the airport in no time.

Why didn't they do that before? Why did I have to go through the manager? I don't know, but I'll tell you this. I'll rent from National every single time because I am convinced that if I have a problem, they are going to take care of it, even if I have to fight them a little bit for it.

People shop at retailers they trust. Look at any consumer survey. You see how important trust is to shoppers. So this is one of the big ways you create Advocates, especially creating Advocates out of Ho-Hums.

Do you want more Advocates in your business? I'm not standing by you right now, but I think you are not answering my question by saying, "No, Art, I've plenty of Advocates, those customers who shop at my store more often and spend more money. What I want to do now is develop some Adversaries who will chase customers away from me, so if you can tell me how to irritate customers, I'd sure appreciate it." Yes, I can sure do that because I've probably irritated my share of them over the years in a whole bunch of different ways.

As I say, though, I think you want more Advocates. Since that's the way you want it, I have some more questions for you: How often do you explain to your employees the importance of creating Advocates with every single customer interaction? How often do you coach your employees on the importance of greeting every customer with an open-ended question, to open up discussion. Greet the customer with, "May I help you?," and eight out of ten say, "No." If we want to turn that around to only three out of ten who say to leave them alone, ask them one of those questions to get them involved. What are you working on today? What do you have going on today? What project do you have going today? What product can I take you to? What aisle can I take you to? Where can I take you to in the store? Get them talking.

Some employees think it is fine to say to a customer, "Well, if you need help, I'll be right over here stocking the tote. Come and find me." But wouldn't you prefer to have those employees working at the competition instead of in your store? Now follow this. It's a little bit subliminal. If I come into your store and your employee greets me by, "May I help you?" and I say no, I'm left there thinking he's wanting to continue to work on what he's working on, and that's where his mind is focused. But if he'd asked me what project I'll be working on, and I said I'm going to be painting my bathroom, what's going through that employee's mind? What color paint will Art want? What else will he need, like rollers, masking tape, drop cloths. I've trained and coached my employees on related-item selling. We want to make the larger sale, and we want the customer to have everything they need to get the project done. I talk about insurance, and here is what I mean by that: If the customer says, "I'm caulking the bathtub and think I need two tubes of caulk," we'll say, "As insurance, get three. If you don't use the third, you can always return it unopened."

Another way we create Advocates is to say thank you. We're in the paint department, and I get the customer everything he's going to need. Now I'm going to release him to the register so I can help the next customer waiting for me. I do my three-part thank you. "Thanks for coming in. I sure appreciate your business. Here's my business card. Call me if you have any questions. Next time you're back in the store, look me up. I want to find out how your project turned out. If you think of it, bring in a couple of photos of what it looks like." The first part of the three-part thank you was the straight out thanks for coming in. The second part was letting the customer know how much we appreciate their business and encouraging them to come back soon and often. That's what at Retail In Motion, LLC, we call Boomerang Customer Service. Have your customers come back soon and often. The third part is the connection. I want to connect with my customer, so I customize a comment to their project or something else that lets that customer know I'm relating to them as a valued individual.

If your store does contractor/trade business, you know what I mean. It is all about relationships. Ace has as retailer in Arizona, Peter, a great guy, a $50 million a year retailer, does a lot of lumber/timber, a lot of contractor/trade business. Home Depot opened up across the street. He took a big hit in his Do It Yourself walk-in traffic but did not drop one dime in the contractor business. It is a matter of relationships. Of course, a lot of that walk-in traffic is good business, so trust me on this one, Peter did not sit around waiting to get that business back. He marketed very, very hard to those DIY customers to get them back in the store. One key to his success in doing that will be the number of Advocates he created before the Home Depot hit.

From the employee side, it is a matter of where you put your priorities. How high a priority do you put on customer service that dazzles the customer? How high a priority do you place on what I call tasks, like unloading those totes, cleaning the floors, and changing the light bulbs? Now you need to get the tasks done, but if you put a higher priority on tasks than on service, you are not going to improve your profitability, believe me.

Putting a higher priority on task than on service is the Big Box mentality. It goes along with what we call Seagull Management. The way this works is that the district manager flies into town, goes into the store, grabs hold of the store manager, flies out on the floor, dumps a whole lot of crud on the store manager, and then flies out of town. Then the store manager goes into his office, gets out his to-do list, writes down everything the district manager said, and he puts it in a nice organized way because he has three senior staff out on the floor, so he flies out onto the floor, and he grabs hold of each one of the senior managers, one at a time, and he drops all kinds of crud on the senior managers before flying back into his office. The senior members of management go into their offices, and they write a hit list for all of their employees, and now we're down to the hourly level. They write it all down and fly out on the floor and drop all kinds of crud on those hourly employees, and then they fly back into their offices. Now you've got an hourly employee who has a list of to-do's a mile long, and do they relate to service or task? It's all task. Not service. With Seagull Management, what message are you giving your staff?

Look over the to-do lists you and your managers hand out in your store. Where on those lists is the priority on customer service, the number one most powerful tactic in improving your profitability through retail pricing? Please keep in mind what I've discussed before: Only retailers who execute legendary customer service deserve to maximize their profitability. You must earn the right to maximize your profitability, and the way you earn your right is by servicing the customer beyond anybody else in the industry.

A while back, I was in a retailer's store on a Saturday from 10:00 AM until noon. Saturday morning. A great time to build sales and build Advocates. I'm walking every one of the aisles in the store. That's all I'm doing because Monday morning, I'm going to be sitting in front of their senior staff members, and I want to be able to talk to them intelligently about their store. And so I walk through the store, and I make eye contact with thirteen employees in the store, thirteen employees. Do you know how many of them said anything to me? One. And that one didn't say much at all.

I'm not saying they weren't doing anything. Every single one of those people was right on task building end caps, stocking merchandise, putting up signs, and absolutely 100% ignoring the customers in the business. So I sat down with the management team, it was Monday morning at 8:00 AM, and I threw a slide onto the screen that says SERVICE OR TASK? I ask them, "What is your priority in your business?" And every one of them, to a man, pounded on their chest like retailers do and said, "Service." Well, I said, "No it's not. You're not even close to being service-oriented. You are all about task." I looked them right in the eyes, and then I told them exactly what happened on Saturday, and I said I definitely did not think it was a fluke. They weren't focusing on tasks because they wanted to get the store all spruced up for me coming to town. No, task was where they were focusing every day.

How many times have you gone out on the floor and talked to the people who work with you about the way they handle a customer out on the floor? How many times have you gone out and given your employees credit for handling a customer exactly the way you thought they should be doing it? How many times have you given an employee constructive criticism, helping them discover the ways to dazzle the customer?

What we have is a tendency to go out there and talk about the task. If you tell me that customer service is your number one priority, the first thing I want to see is your job description. You hired me, what do you want me to do? Take care of the customer or do the task? Maybe you'll say it's a little bit of both, but when I'm your employee, and I have to choose between service and task, what does the job description say I should do?

After I look over the job description, I want to see your performance appraisal forms. What do you evaluate your people on? How much on service, how much on task? Where is the priority? Are you evaluating your people on how they deal with the customer or are you evaluating them on how fast they can put away stock, how well they do with signage, how many tasks they can get done in a day?

There are businesses that are very successful picking task as a priority. Bunning's in Australia is clearly task-related.

Home Depot and Lowe's in the U.S. That's their business model. That's what works for them. For us, you and me, the small to midsize retail business, it's all about service. The next time you're walking the floor of your store, please think about what I'm saying here. Think about how much time you spend in a day down on the sales floor watching an employee and the way they deal with the customers and listening to the customers. Then when they get done, either give them credit for doing it very well or constructive criticism for not doing it quite as well as you thought they should be doing it.

The second most important thing in the store, next to being in-stock, is that interaction. I also would argue that we have a tendency to *tell* our people, but we don't *train* them enough, and we don't *coach* them enough. We don't give them all the tools they need when we don't train them or continue to coach them. I'm not big into scripting everything for the employees, telling them just what to say in every situation, but I am big into scripting a few things in the store. For example, if you've read this far, you know that I don't think you should leave it to chance on how people in your store greet the customer. I don't think you should leave it to chance on how they thank the customer, I don't think you should leave it to chance on how they answer the telephone, and in my opinion there should be scripts for all those.

When it comes to Boomerang Customer Service, your store is only as good as the weakest staff member a customer might come into contact with. I'll give you an example. I did a retailer meeting at a DoubleTree Inn, which is a Hilton property. I checked in about 4:00 in the afternoon, and the woman behind the counter was outstanding. Just outstanding. I went to dinner that night, and when I came back by the front desk, the woman greeted me with, "Good night, Mr. Freedman." Just superb. Very good so far. I went to sleep loving the DoubleTree Inn in Livermore.

I like to get an early start in the morning to make sure everything is working in my meeting room. I've had everything go wrong that can go wrong with a computer and a projector, and I know that if I have an hour, I can get most things fixed. I walk down to the front desk, where there's now a different woman on duty, and I ask her where my meeting room is located. She points down a hallway and tells me to go down that way. I don't like employees in my store who point to an aisle instead of walking the customer there, so my first reaction to the woman pointing is sort of a chill inside me. But I figure I can stand it because it is early morning and maybe the woman needs to be at the front desk.

So I walk down the hallway to the room, only to find that it is locked. I walk back to the counter, where the woman is sitting there reading a newspaper. I say, "Can you please open the door to that meeting room? It's locked." She tosses the newspaper down and says, "Well, I guess if I have to." Okay, whatever. She meets me in the hallway, and as we're walking towards where the meeting room is, I say, "Am I asking you to do something that you're not supposed to do?" I figure that's a fair question, and I was interested in what she'd say. Her answer: "Well, you know, I was busy."

Busy reading a newspaper? Well, I don't need to tell you what happened to my perception of that DoubleTree Inn. I changed from Advocate to at most Ho-Hum, and maybe even Adversary. I'm not at all ready to recommend that hotel to anybody, and if anybody asked me what I thought of that hotel, I'd tell them about my bad experience there.

For me, a lesson from all that is you need consistency in the customer service in your store. That's because customer service is so important for our profitability. Customers forgive the Big Boxes for bad customer service, but they don't forgive us.

You know how it plays out in your world. I'll tell you how it played out in my world. A customer comes into the store with a whole bag of plumbing fittings, throws them out on the counter, and looks very frustrated. He says, "What am I supposed to do with this stuff?" I ask, "What are you trying to do?" He says, "Well, I've got a half-inch compression, and

I need to go to half-inch iron pipe." And I go, "Oh, okay," and I walk over to where I have that stuff, show it to him, and show him how it works, and that's it right there. Then he walks back to the counter again and says, "How about all this other stuff? What am I supposed to do with it?" And I go, "I see the Home Depot bag it came in. Why not take it back over there and ask *them*?" The customer says, "I am not ever going back to Home Depot. Ever." So you say, okay, thanks. Fine. Everything's done. The customer is out of the store.

Two weeks later, I'm over at Home Depot, and I'm walking around the store just checking it out, and who do I see? There's that same customer. I go up and say, "You told me a couple of weeks ago you were never going to come over here again. I helped you with that fitting. What are you doing?" And this is what that customer says, "You know, they are so big here, and they don't have very many employees in the store because they're trying to keep the costs down, and I just thought I'd give them another chance." And those customers do it over and over again. That's how it works because otherwise how did Home Depot get to be a $90 billion company (lower now since selling off part of the company) irritating customers? You can't do it. The strength of the Big Boxes is all about assortment and price and really not a lot to do with the whole customer service equation.

The Big Boxes are saying they really want to get back to helping the customers in the store. I'm saying they are never going to get there. It's a spin, a promotion in the marketplace, but they're never going to get there. Their turnover rate of employees in each store is just too high to be able to execute good customer service, and if they find somebody who is good, you know what they do with them? They move them up the ladder very quickly. That's their business model again.

The high turnover rate affects not just customer service, but also the Services element in our Retail Pyramid of Profit. In the market area of my store, there are not many locksmiths to rekey locks and no specialty shops to do rescreening, window repair, blade sharpening, or the rest. Can the Big Boxes do it reliably? No. When you have annual employee turnover as high as they have, think what happens. They get an employee trained on rekeying a lock, and two weeks later the employee is gone. They can't do it, so my store grabs hold of as many services as possible that are done in a community.

My definition of services is pretty wide. What do you test? Things like batteries, pool water, soil, water heater elements, range elements. What do you fix? The biggest thing we fix is the stupid weed eater because customers keep getting that stupid spool jammed up. We customize. We sell by the foot. Big Boxes don't like to sell by the foot. In our store, we have about 575 SKUs that are cut. We cut wire, tubing, pipe, and so on. A total of 575 items. A typical Home Depot has less than half as many.

I'd much rather say yes to a customer and put a price on it than to say no. There are some people who would say why in the world would a customer come to American River Ace Hardware, buy a pallet of concrete, and have it delivered across the street? It's going to cost twice as much as it would at Home Depot. But if they want me to do it, I'll do it. A lot of our customers have accounts in the store. They don't want to go over to Home Depot. They want to come here to take care of business. They are American River Ace Hardware Advocates, and they love us. Why would a customer give us $250 extra for a Weber barbecue? Well, they'll want us to take it up to their home in Lake Tahoe, about 90 miles away, set it up in their backyard, see that it's hooked to a full tank of propane, and it is ready to go. Well, if they ask, we're going to do it. But we're not going to do it for free. It is far better and more profitable to say yes to a customer and apply a price to it than it is to say no.

Some of my employees might say, "With what I earn, I wouldn't pay that much extra, so I'm not going to suggest it to the customer." I look at those employees and say, "There are people who come into this store who have a lot of money. They are willing to pay to hear the word yes and know that we will do what we say we'll do. They don't care if we charge them $250 to get the Weber barbeque up to Lake Tahoe. They just want us to say yes.

All of this gives us other opportunities to be world-class for the customer and be distinctive from our competitors. That's an advantage we can have.

It only works, though, when we keep our priorities at Top-of-Mind Awareness for ourselves and for our employees. What comes first, service or task? You have got to know that it is SERVICE. When does the value of an item exceed the value of a customer? You've got to know that the answer is NEVER. This goes back to what I discussed before about refunds, exchanges, and exceptions.

Ace Hardware Corporation has people on staff to take phone calls, emails, and letters from customers who hate or love Ace. They get thousands of these contacts each year. Research says that only about 10% of the Adversaries will take the time to tell you what they don't like, so I figure that putting it all together for everybody flying the Ace banner, we're managing to really irritate loads of people every year.

A very high percentage of the complaints coming to Ace Hardware Corporation are on how we handle refunds and product exchanges. Here's one true tale: A customer goes into an Ace Hardware store on the East Coast one weekend. His purchase comes out to $487.62 with a garbage disposal, light fixtures, and that kind of stuff. The man goes home, and on Monday and Tuesday, as I understand what happened, he installs everything. He finds that he has a clamp left over. It's a 29¢ clamp. That Friday, he goes back into the store on his way home from work. He shops through the store and buys more stuff to work on his project some more over the weekend. After the cashier rings it all up, he says something like, "Oh, by the way, I need to return this cable clamp." The cashier says, "Do you have your receipt?" He pulls it out, and she looks for the 29¢ item on the receipt so she can circle it. Then she says, "You know, we sell those in a plastic bag so we can scan them. Do you have your plastic bag with you?"

Hey, I know this is painful for you to read. Think how painful it is for me to write it. It cuts into me like a knife. We might want to not even believe it. Well, okay, I'm making up some of what was said between the cashier and the customer since I wasn't right there at the time, but it did go pretty much like this: The cashier asks the customer to show her the plastic bag that came with this 29¢ item before she'll credit him with his 29¢, and he says, "No, I don't have the plastic bag." The cashier says, "I think we've got a problem." Well at this point I'm thinking there is a problem, a big problem, but it is with the store, with the store management.

The man says, "I don't have a problem. Call your manager." The on-duty manager comes to the register and says to the cashier, "What's the problem?" Don't ever do that. Go up to the register and say, "What do we need to do to take care of this?," or, "What do we need to do to make this right?," like that manager at National Car Rental said to me. Here, though, the manager asks, "What's the problem," and the cashier says, "This customer is trying to return this cable clamp, and he doesn't have the plastic bag." The manager says to the customer, "Do you have your plastic bag?" What a useless, disrespectful question to this guy who spent almost $500 the last weekend and just had another purchase rung up.

The customer answers, "No, I don't have the plastic bag." The he takes his items and walks out of the store. Next day, he contacts the store owner and the day after that, he's in the store owner's office with everything he had bought. He returns everything he had bought. He takes his loyalty club card and cuts it all up, hands it to the guy, and says, "I'll never be inside your store again," and he walks away. This guy had been spending over $5,000 a year in this store, and they turned him away over a plastic bag.

The cashier thought she was helping out the store owner. Hourly employees think they are helping out when they say no. Maybe they are saying it because they like the power of saying no. I think that's one of the reasons it happens. Also, it is easier to say no than to go through what you need to do if you say yes. But hourly employees don't understand the power of the brand, even when we train them about it. I would like you to think about putting this in place in your store for your hourly employees: If you can't say yes to a customer on a return, you are not allowed to say no. Only the senior member of management on staff at any given time is allowed to say no to the customer on a return.

When you tell a customer no on a return, you have fired them. Customers cost us a fortune to get, a fortune. I have seen a customer turned away because they brought a $20 hammer to the store after the customer hammered it into concrete, and the head broke off, and the hourly employee tells the customer no on a return. I thought, "You have got to be kidding me." Do you know what they're saying when they do that? Very simple. That hammer is more important than you. That's exactly what they're saying, and I do get emotional about it because I've seen what happens at retailers around the world, and it will absolutely kill a company.

Frequently number one across all levels of customer service in the U.S. is Nordstrom. That department store will take anything back. There are legends told about Nordstrom that say they don't even care if they're the one who sold you the item. One story is about a guy who brought back four tires to Nordstrom. All they want to know is how much did he pay for the tires so they could give him the right refund amount. If you ask Nordstrom management why, they'd say, "He's here in our store, he is going to spend some money, and he loves us to death, so he'll be back again and again, and he'll tell everybody he knows to come here to shop."

I've never tried returning my car tires to Nordstrom, but I'll tell you a story that I know from personal experience did happen: John goes into Nordstrom and buys a $100 shirt. After he wears the shirt a few times, he takes it into the cleaners. When John picks up the laundered shirt from the cleaners and takes it home, he sees that the laundry scorched his shirt. "No problem," says his wife. "Next time we are in Nordstrom, we will get you another." "Why?," says John. "It wasn't their fault." "Do not even think twice about this John," states his wife. The next time they are in Nordstrom, John meekly presents his scorched shirt to a sales person. The sales person holds up the shirt and says "Oh, your cleaners scorched the shirt." John says, "My wife made me bring it back." "Hold on a second," says the salesperson. He leaves for a minute and returns with a new shirt. "Will this one work for you, sir?" "Yes, it will work! I can wear this one. But this wasn't your fault. Why are you doing this? Is it your job?" Says the salesperson, "Not only is it my job to service you, sir, it is my pleasure."

When you say you are good at customer service, are you *that* good?

Have I ever had to say no to a customer? You bet I have. Have I ever had to fire a customer? You I bet I have, and so will you. But I would like to think that decision is going to be made at your level and not by a new employee who just came into the store and who doesn't understand the power of the brand.

A customer walks in the front door, they walk to the tool department, they steal something, put it in their pocket, and walk out. They come into the store again, go to the service desk, set the item down on the service desk, and say, "I need to get my money back on this." In my store, the cashier will not say no. The cashier will call the manager over. The manager says, "When did you purchase the item?" The customer says, "Yesterday." The manager goes into the computer, looks at the customer, and says, "I cannot verify this right now. I need to verify this before I give you a refund without a receipt. Please give me your name and address so when I verify this, I will mail you a refund."

We are not ever going to mail out that refund because we're not ever going to be able to verify the purchase. But we've got the product back, we absolutely diffused any problem at the front end of the store, and the customer is gone. That's one where I don't want that customer returning to my store. He's fired, and it is perfectly okay with me. We call that whole thing a check refund, and we use that concept for items we know the customer stole, they know they stole it, everybody knows they stole it, and we need to get them out of the store so they won't be yelling at us at the front register.

Refunds are an emotional topic. I know it. Man, do retailers like to take sides on this one! When you get together and talk retail, you'll hear how every single person in that room has been burned by a customer before. I've been burned by the best of them. But you know what? If I get ripped off for $100, I'll be out there playing my margins to get the $100 back. I'm not going to worry about it. If you're getting ripped off all the time on refunds, okay, you've got to tighten things up. That's shrinkage, and we've talked about that. But if the rip-off is the exception, don't fire the customer. When you fire a customer, they don't stop being a customer, they just stop being your customer. You've created an Adversary, maybe turned a Ho-Hum or an Advocate into an Adversary, and you know what trouble that turns out to be. The least expensive way to handle an upset customer is to give them their money back. The most expensive way is to lose them as an Advocate or potential Advocate.

## GOLDEN NUGGETS FOR NOW

- Whenever you want to improve the perception your customers have of your pricing, improve your customer service.
- Pay close attention to how well your store is developing Advocates who will recommend your store to others.
- Train your staff to respond to irritated customers by asking, "What can I do to make this right?"
- Do all you can to build customer trust, keeping in mind that people shop at retailers they trust.
- Anticipate the customer's needs and offer them insurance: For instance, if the customer

says, "I'm caulking the bathtub and think I need two tubes of caulk," say, "As insurance, get three. If you don't use the third, you can always return it unopened."

- Set the nonnegotiable standard that every staff member will thank each customer by saying something like, "Thanks for coming in. I sure appreciate your business. Here's my business card. Call me if you have any questions. Next time you're back in the store, look me up. I want to find out how your project turned out. If you think of it, bring in a couple of photos of what it looks like."

- In every interaction you have with staff, keep the primary focus on how well they're delivering customer service, not on how well they are accomplishing the store tasks.

- Use scripts to help employees know how to greet the customer, thank the customer, and answer the telephone.

- Each day, remind yourself and your staff, "Customers forgive the Big Boxes for bad customer service, but they don't forgive us."

- Whenever possible, say yes to a customer and apply a price to satisfying that customer request.

- Insist that a customer can be fired only by the most senior level person on duty in the store. Set as a nonnegotiable standard for floor staff that the value of an item NEVER exceeds the value of a customer. The least expensive way to handle an upset customer is to give them their money back. The most expensive way is to lose them as an Advocate or potential Advocate.

- Use a check refund in situations where you know the customer stole an item and you want to get them out of the store so they won't be yelling by the front register: Say, "I cannot verify this right now. I need to verify this before I give you a refund without a receipt. Please give me your name and address so when I verify this, I will mail you a refund." You are not ever going to mail out that refund because you're not ever going to be able to verify the purchase.

- Build customer trust because your customers, just like you and me, prefer to shop with retailers we trust.

# CHAPTER 10: NOW GO DO IT

*Can anybody remember when the times were not hard
and money not scarce?*
Ralph Waldo Emerson (1870)

As Bruce Sanders and I are putting this book together in the first months of 2009, retailing is in a worldwide slump. But as you are reading the book, I'd like us, you and I, to see this as a time of promise. Coming out of this economic upheaval, the survivors will be the strong, nimble retailers who have known it is okay to make money. Each day, they walk the aisles of their stores spotting opportunities, hundreds of potentials for building their business.

I grew up in the retail discount world from 1966 to 1974. It was in 1974 that I moved into the retail hardware/home center segment. Over those years, I have worked for only a few companies. Some had weak leadership, and they failed. I've also worked with a couple, including my current co-op, which have strong leadership. The ones with strong leadership taught me from my early years in retailing to walk every single aisle every single workday. And I can easily tell you what I'm looking for, since I've done it for so many years. It is one of the first things I teach in the first week to any manager who works for me. First off, are we in-stock? Second, I'm looking at the customer-staff interaction. Then I'm looking at the displays, the signing, and the housekeeping.

I can imagine you saying, "Well, what do you mean, walk every aisle every day? Things don't change every day." If you are saying that, my answer is, "You've got to be kidding me. Not only do things change every day, and I don't care what volume you're doing, but every time you walk the floor, you see something different."

The last item I'm always looking at is, "How are we getting ready to be even better than we are now?" How much time every week do you spend planning to be better? I would hope you'd have an answer for me. It should be right on top of your head, right there. Here's what we're doing every day. Here's what we're doing every week. Here's what we're doing every month to be better because that is how great retailers build their businesses. They've built the business by getting a little bit better every day. You know what? If you are looking for the one great idea, the one thing that will take you from here to there, that one absolutely phenomenal idea, it doesn't exist any more. It's not out there. We'd be looking for something that is not there anymore. What we need to do now as competition gets tougher and tougher and tougher is to make little baby steps every single day so that at the end of the week, we're that much better, and at the end of the month, we're even better.

I asked you at the start of this book to please do just a few things differently. Do them well, and that will make the time you've spent reading this book worthwhile. Then you can build from there.

The top two reasons that the owners of small to midsize retail businesses do not make more money is that they lack the courage it takes and the ability to make the tough decisions. Thank you very much for joining me and for thinking about the golden nuggets. I really appreciate it. But now's the time to go beyond thinking to doing. Go out there and make more money.

The value of any business book I have read can be measured in two ways: Entertainment and, more importantly, can I use the information to get results? The content of this book is real-world stuff that can produce results when implemented and followed through by people who believe in improving their businesses. Many of the golden nuggets have been implemented by our stores, and they have gotten results. Many of them require guts to implement and to hold the line, but the rewards are worth it. In a competitive environment, the need for practical, useful, and easy-to-implement strategies and tactics has never been greater. There are lots of them in this book.

JOHN ENGLISH
GROUP GENERAL MANAGER
SALES & MEMBER SERVICES
MITRE 10 AUSTRALIA, LTD.

Finally, a book by a retailer for retailers! General business books always have one or two things that you can apply to your business. Everything in this book is directly applicable. Art's nuggets are proven money-makers that he has generously laid out in a straightforward manner. Read, implement, and start making more money today.

MARYANNE & CHARLES G. BIDDIX, OWNERS
PALMETTO ACE HOME CENTER
PAWLEYS ISLAND, SOUTH CAROLINA

At a minimum, this book is a must read for every hardware store owner and manager. We all know how the old saying goes: "If you get only one idea out of it, it was worth it." That saying does not apply to this book because you are guaranteed to get five ideas out of it, and that's if you don't even try. Art puts "How to make money" in words and examples that can't be duplicated by any lawyer, accountant, or business consultant. The bottom line is that this book will put real money on YOUR bottom line.

PAT BOWMAN, OWNER
R.W. HINE ACE HARDWARE
CHESHIRE, CONNECTICUT

We are the largest auto parts distributor in the Republic of South Africa, operating 167 AutoZone stores, and the largest member-owned Do It Yourself hardware retailer in the country, operating 180 stores under the Mica brand. Unlike with so many other books for retailers, the ideas in Art and Bruce's book come from the reality of retailing. Whilst Art's experience is primarily as a hardware retailer, we've also exposed our auto parts business to the ideas in this book, and the unanimous response has been that this is real take-home value to the organisation.
PETER GRANAT, CEO
SUPER GROUP RETAIL SUPPLY CHAIN
REPUBLIC OF SOUTH AFRICA

When you read Making Money Is Not Illegal, Immoral, or Fattening, you will find an abundance of good ideas. Read the book, execute the ideas, and make more money in your business.
RICH LAWRENCE, OWNER/OPERATOR
EMIGH ACE HARDWARE
SACRAMENTO, CALIFORNIA

Perhaps the most significant nugget I gained from reading this book was my realisation that I had a great retail offer, I just needed to be brave enough to charge the customer what it was worth. I was afraid to make money. Now using Art's margin management strategies, we have completely transformed our business. It feels so good to make a buck. I am a margin junky, and I am enjoying my job again.
MIKE COATES, OWNER
COATES MITRE 10 HOME & TRADE
LITHGOW NSW, AUSTRALIA

This isn't another self help book. If you apply these basic principles, results will follow. Art's book is easy to read, easy to apply, and WILL improve your results. Grains of sand make a beach, and Art provides everything except the umbrella.
DOUG WRIGHT
GENERAL MANAGER/VICE PRESIDENT, OPERATIONS

MOUNTAIN HARDWARE AND SPORTS
TRUCKEE, CALIFORNIA

Art and Bruce tell great stories to make their points, and when Art talks about margin management, he gets to the heart of how to make a highly profitable difference in your retail business. Art Freedman is an inspirational presenter in person and the written word. This book is a must for all retailers.
JIM COPELAND, CHIEF EXECUTIVE
IRISH HARDWARE & BUILDING MATERIALS ASSOCIATION

Wow, great book. You have hit on many issues that face retailers today. Making Money Is Not Illegal, Immoral, or Fattening is stimulating and informative. It makes a retailer think retail! Most small retailers are more reactive than proactive, and reading your book makes a dealer more proactive. This is not an all-or-nothing book. You can pick out ideas that help you based on where you are in your business.
MARTIN RUGGIERO, PRESIDENT
JANT GROUPS, INC.
UNITED STATES

I expect that any retailer in any country can apply Art's retail strategies and make more money in their business.
PAULUS ONG, DIRECTOR
ACE HARDWARE AND INDEX FURNISHING
INDONESIA

Please see www.retailinmotion.us for the range of services and products available from Retail In Motion, LLC to improve retailer profitability, all of them ready to be customized for your particular business needs. Our tools include results-focused workshops, seminars, conference keynotes, consulting, mentoring, and multimedia skills development.

Art Freedman provides retailer-to-retailer services, with an emphasis on retail finance, margin management, successfully competing with the Big Boxes, and maintaining top-of-mind awareness with your customers and potential customers. Art has more than forty years experience in retailing, during which he has held job positions that range from hourly clerk through multi-store owner. Art has delivered real-world training and mentoring to more than 500 groups, touching more than 15,000 retailers. He's presented in every U.S. state and in more than 20 other countries.

Bruce Sanders, Ph.D., SPHR, is an organizational and consumer psychologist who also is certified as a Senior Professional in Human Resources. Bruce provides retail management training and consultation throughout the world, with an emphasis on boosting sales, human resource management, systems improvement, technology utilization, and retail store leadership. His workshops have been praised for combining university-quality accuracy with hands-on tactics that retailers can put right to use.